Boogers Are
My Beat

*Also by Dave Barry
in Large Print:*

Big Trouble
Dave Barry Is Not Taking
   This Sitting Down!
Dave Barry Turns 50
Tricky Business

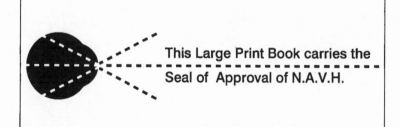

Boogers Are My Beat

More Lies,
but Some Actual Journalism

Dave Barry

Thorndike Press • Waterville, Maine

Copyright © 2003 by Dave Barry

The essays in this work have appeared previously
in the *Miami Herald*.

Published in 2004 by arrangement with Crown Publishers, a
division of Random House, Inc.

Thorndike Press® Large Print Core.

The tree indicium is a trademark of Thorndike Press.

The text of this Large Print edition is unabridged.
Other aspects of the book may vary from the original edition.

Set in 16 pt. Plantin.

Printed in the United States on permanent paper.

Library of Congress Cataloging-in-Publication Data

Barry, Dave.
    Boogers are my beat : more lies, but some actual
journalism / Dave Barry.
        p. cm.
    ISBN 0-7862-6193-5 (lg. print : hc : alk. paper)
    1. American wit and humor. 2. Large type books.
I. Title.
PN6165.B37 2003b
    814'.54—dc22   2003068680

Boogers Are My Beat

As the Founder/CEO of NAVH, the only national health agency solely devoted to those who, although not totally blind, have an eye disease which could lead to serious visual impairment, I am pleased to recognize Thorndike Press* as one of the leading publishers in the large print field.

Founded in 1954 in San Francisco to prepare large print textbooks for partially seeing children, NAVH became the pioneer and standard setting agency in the preparation of large type.

Today, those publishers who meet our standards carry the prestigious "Seal of Approval" indicating high quality large print. We are delighted that Thorndike Press is one of the publishers whose titles meet these standards. We are also pleased to recognize the significant contribution Thorndike Press is making in this important and growing field.

Lorraine H. Marchi, L.H.D.
Founder/CEO
NAVH

* Thorndike Press encompasses the following imprints: Thorndike, Wheeler, Walker and Large Print Press.

Contents

Introduction:
Boogers Are My Beat

I'm not a real journalist. I'm a humor columnist. When real journalists are out interviewing experts about important issues such as terrorism and the economy, I'm at home, sitting in front of my computer in my underwear, trying to decide which animal name is funnier, "hamster" or "gerbil."[1]

But because I work for a major newspaper, *The Miami Herald*,[2] I sometimes get to go to major news events, such as political conventions, the Olympics, Elizabeth Taylor fragrance launches, etc. My usual tactic at such events is to lurk among the real journalists as they interview a newsmaker. I frown thoughtfully at the newsmaker and write stuff in my notebook, just like my media colleagues; the difference is that

[1] Answer: "weasel."
[2] Motto: "Serving a Vibrant Community of Two Million People, of Whom Twenty-three Speak English."

they're writing down what the newsmaker is saying, whereas I'm writing notes like, "GREEN THING STUCK IN TEETH" or "NOSE SIZE OF EGGPLANT."

Over the past two decades, I've used this tactic to cover dozens of major national and international news events, and I've written hundreds of columns about them. When my editor, Betty Prashker, and I were putting this book together, we decided to take a look back at those older columns to see if any of them were worth including here. What we found, frankly, surprised us: Despite the fact that those columns concerned, in some cases, events that took place years ago, a surprising number of them, when viewed from the perspective of recent events, are — and I say this in all modesty — complete gibberish. They're filled with obscure references to people who, at one time, apparently were quite famous for some reason, but whose names no longer ring a bell. "Al Gore," for example.

So Betty and I threw most of the columns out. But there were some that we thought would be worth including, and we've started the book with those. Toward the end of the book we've included some more recent columns, so you can judge how much I have matured as a writer. Actually, I can just tell you here: I have not matured at all. Thank God. Maturity is a crippling handicap for humor columnists. It's like height for jockeys, or ethics for lawyers.

The first section of this book presents some columns I wrote about presidential politics, which, in my professional opinion, is the mother lode of humor material. We have a lot of funny institutions in this country — infomercials, California, Al Sharpton, organized religion — but for consistently wacky hijinks, you cannot beat the way we go about choosing our maximum leader.

I've been covering presidential politics since 1984, when the *Herald* sent me to New Hampshire to write about the presidential primaries. I went up there and wrote about what goes on in the New Hampshire primary; namely, a bunch of candidates in dark suits, accompanied by dark-suited entourages, race frantically around the state, grasping voters' hands and telling them — with all the sincerity of a guy in a bar declaring his love to a woman he met three drinks earlier — how deeply they care about New Hampshire.

I thought my reports were pretty accurate, but not everybody at the *Herald* liked them. I was especially criticized for one column about a campaign appearance by Sen. John Glenn, in which I pointed out that he was not an electrifying speaker. I believe my exact words were: "He could not electrify a fish tank if he threw a toaster into it."

This column angered a member of the *Herald*'s editorial board.[3] He was a serious journalist, and he wrote a serious memo to our executive editor, objecting to my coverage of the primary campaign. The memo said: "When we treat so prominently such serious business as if it were pratfall comedy, I believe that we demean our reputation as a serious newspaper. I seriously believe that such treatment reassures the public that cynicism about politics is smart."

Well, heaven forbid that we journalists should make the public cynical about politics. But having covered five presidential campaigns, I frankly do not know what you could write about our political process that would make it appear any stupider than it actually is.

[3.] The editorial board is a group of newspaper employees who go into a room every single day and form strong opinions. The rest of us employees do not know how they do this. We suspect a "Magic 8 Ball" is involved.

Of course when we think about the words "stupid" and "politics" together, we naturally think about the 2000 presidential election, especially the role played by my state, Florida.[4] We'll begin this book with some columns I wrote during that hideous period when the entire world was waiting to find out who the next U.S. president would be, while haggard Florida election officials squinted at chads, and squadrons of lawyers dropped from the sky.[5]

What follows is a series of columns I wrote for the *Herald* about that election. The first one, which appeared the day after Election Day, was an "analysis" of the election results. The joke was supposed to be that I wrote this analysis without knowing who the winner was. Little did I realize that this would still be a mystery *weeks* after this column appeared.

That column is followed by some more about the election mess, followed by one on the inauguration of George W. Bush, an event that gave a new definition[6] to the word "fun."

— Dave Barry

4. Motto: "Florida — You Can't Spell It Without 'Duh.' "
5. Tragically, most of them were wearing parachutes.
6. Specifically, "not fun."

A Wacky Path for Politics

Memo: ELECTION 2000

Before I analyze the presidential election, I want to make a statement, on behalf of South Florida, to the state and local candidates who ran all those TV ads, especially Elaine Bloom, Clay Shaw, Bill McCollum, and Bill Nelson: We hope that you and all your media advisers rot in Campaign Hell, okay? We hope that demons tape your eyelids open and force you to watch your own TV commercials. We hope that every thousand years, the demons hold an election to decide which one of you should be allowed to leave Campaign Hell, and the winner is always: None of the Above.

There! I feel better! Now, let's analyze the presidential election. As you can imagine, I was up all night scrutinizing the returns. (NOTE TO EDITOR: The truth is, I'm writing this while the polls are still open. I don't plan to watch the returns. I plan to watch *Buffy the Vampire Slayer* and be asleep by 9:15 P.M. So I need some help finishing this analysis.)

The key to presidential elections is the Electoral College, an institution created by the Founding Fathers so that Tim Russert would have something to talk about. Under this system, each state receives a certain number of electoral votes, based on how stupid the state's motto is. Thus, New York (motto: "Driver Carries No Cash") has 33 electoral votes; whereas North Dakota (motto: "Coming Soon — Plumbing!") has none.

This system can produce some quirky results. In 1884, the Electoral College declared that Grover Cleveland was the winner, even though it turned out that there was no such person. Later, the Electoral College got a bee in its bonnet and elected Franklin D. Roosevelt president twenty-seven times in a row. Still later, it elected Richard M. Nixon, despite abundant documented evidence that he was Richard M. Nixon.

So the Electoral College may seem to be a wacky way to elect a president. But it's better than any other system on earth, except the system we use to fill every other office. And because of this system, one of the keys to Tuesday's election was the 25 electoral votes of Florida (motto: "Drugs

Are Legal, but God Help You If You Get Caught with a Citrus Tree!").

To win Florida, both candidates needed the support of our 398 million elderly residents, all of whom vote. Voting is one of their major forms of entertainment, along with eating dinner at 4:30 P.M. and failing to notice green lights while sitting behind the wheels of their 1986 Oldsmobiles. To win the votes of these people, both Al Gore and George W. Bush promised that, if elected, they would have the government give the elderly huge quantities of drugs. So one definite outcome of the election is that, for the next four years, our seniors, God bless them, will be stoned out of their gourds. This will probably improve their driving.

But the elderly vote was only one of many factors that determined the outcome of the election, which is why all the experts said it was "too close to call." What a bunch of morons. I predicted the outcome of this election right on the money in a column I wrote on April 17, 1997. My exact words were: "The next president of the United States will definitely be (NOTE TO EDITOR: Please insert the winner's name here)."

The question now is: What lies ahead for

the nation, with this man at the helm? What kind of a man IS this man, assuming that he is, in fact, a man? The answers will determine the future of this great nation, and we all, as Americans, must think about them very hard. But right now, *Buffy* is starting.

Wrong! It Wasn't Humphrey

We in the news media have an announcement to make.

It turns out we made a few teensy mistakes in our coverage of the presidential election. Oh, we were correct on the big stuff, such as what day the election was held, the names of the candidates, and how many total states there are. But we messed up on some of the minor details, such as who, technically, got elected president.

This happened because, here in the news media, our focus is on speed. When we get hold of some new and possibly inaccurate information, our highest priority is to get it to you, the public, before our competitors do. If the news media owned airlines, there would be a lot less concern about how many planes crashed, and a lot more concern about whose plane hit the ground first.

Nowhere is the speed competition more fierce than in TV news. This is why if you decided — God help you — to stay informed on election night by watching television, you saw the following sequence of events:

- First, the major networks confidently declared, based on a careful analysis of the voting patterns of approximately four people, that Al Gore had won Florida.
- A little while later, the networks announced that — Whoops! — Gore had NOT won Florida.
- Still later, the networks confidently declared that George W. Bush had won Florida, and the presidency.
- Next, the networks explained, in some detail, how Bush had done it, and what he would do as *forty-third* president of the United States.
- Then the networks declared that — Whoops again! — Bush had NOT won Florida.
- Then the networks declared that the World Series was actually won by the Mets.

Okay, I made that last one up. But all the other stuff *actually happened*. In other words, if you had hoped to inform yourself about the most important story in the world by watching network TV news — the most expensive and sophisticated news-gathering operation in history — you actually wound up less informed than if you had spent the night staring at your refrigerator.

I am not saying the newspapers did any better. Oh, we tried to get you the story. We were in constant contact with our news sources. The problem is, our news sources are (Don't tell anybody!) the TV networks. So we were just as confused as anybody else, which is why an early edition of the *Herald* had a front-page headline declaring that the election had been won by the late Hubert Humphrey.

In fact, as I write these words, NOBODY knows who won the presidential election, because nobody knows who won Florida. We're having a recount, which should be pretty entertaining, because Florida's No. 3 industry, behind tourism and skin cancer, is voter fraud. Here in Miami, we've had elections where the dead voters outnumbered the live ones. Elsewhere in the state there have been reports of irregular voting procedures, including one Palm Beach County precinct where the "ballots" given to voters were actually pizza coupons. (As of right now, Extra Cheese holds a slim lead over Pepperoni, but Tim Russert says it is "still too close to call.")

So this election, which the nation had desperately hoped would be over by now, is going to drag on — nobody knows how long — and all because of Florida. We are a REALLY popular state right now. It wouldn't surprise me if, after this is all over, we get voted out of the union. That really would be a shame. Because I think Humphrey is going to make a damned good president.

Why Not Poke a Hole in a Candidate's Eyeball?

I think it's an arrow thing.

I'm talking about this deal with the ballots in Palm Beach County.

As the whole world knows by now, thanks to Florida, the presidential election has come to a grinding halt. Lawsuits are being filed. People are marching in the streets. Political pundits are so excited that they have to change their underwear on an hourly basis. Jesse Jackson has taken time out from his busy schedule of garnering publicity elsewhere so he can devote all his efforts to garnering publicity here.

And the scary part is, nobody knows how long this will drag on. We may not know who our forty-third president is until it's time to elect our forty-fourth.

At the heart of all this mess is Palm Beach County, where many people are now saying they didn't know whom they were voting for. Every time you turn on the news you see distraught Palm Beach voters saying that they accidentally voted for the wrong person, or two people, or nobody, or Queen Elizabeth II.

These people blame the ballot, which they say was very confusing. The way they talk, it sounds as though to understand this ballot, you would need, at minimum, a degree in nuclear physics. Now, I have seen pictures of this ballot. And although I think the design could have been better, it doesn't seem all THAT complicated. I mean, for each candidate's name, there's an arrow pointing to a punch hole. If you follow the arrow, you get to the correct hole, right?

And that's where I think the problem arises. Because, for whatever reason, many people in Florida do NOT understand arrows. If you have ever driven down here, you know what I mean. You'll be at an intersection, waiting in the left-turn lane, with a big painted arrow on the street, pointing left; and a sign overhead saying LEFT TURN ONLY with an arrow pointing left; and then the light will change, and there will be a green arrow, pointing left, and 50 percent of the time the driver in front of you will do . . . nothing! It's as if this driver has NO IDEA what the arrows mean! Sometimes — and if you don't

27

believe me, then you have never driven in South Florida — the driver will attempt to turn RIGHT.

So I think that, given the population down here, it was a big mistake to put arrows on the ballot. It would be better to use a system easier to grasp, such as putting actual photographs of the candidates on the ballot; voters could indicate their preference by using their hole-punchers to poke the candidate of their choice in the eyeball.

For now, though, we need to figure out what to do about this election. Here's what I say we do: I say we take the 25 electoral votes away from Florida and give them to some less-populated but more-deserving state — say Delaware, or North Dakota — that is at least capable of figuring out which candidate it voted for. Do you think this is a good idea? Please take a moment to let me know by punching the correct hole in the ballot below:

I agree with Dave   ➡   ●

I do not agree with Dave   ➡   ●

Okay, I'm tabulating your results now, and the winner is . . . Pat Buchanan. I'm moving to Sweden.

Now It's Time to Say Thanks for the Chads That Don't Count

Boy, am I ever thankful.

I'm talking about Miami-Dade County's decision not to recount its presidential ballots after all.

As you know, in Palm Beach and Broward counties, groups of wretched people have been spending long, dreary days looking at ballots, squinting at pregnant chads, gay and lesbian chads, dimpled chads, freckled chads, Kentucky Fried Chads, the Artist Formerly Known as Chad, etc.

Their goal is to figure out what in God's name the voters were thinking when they did whatever they did to these ballots. This is not easy, because a lot of these voters apparently have the functional IQs of starfish. There's no other way to explain some of the things they did in the voting booth. ("Hey! I think I'll vote for . . .

TWO presidents!")

Don't get me wrong: I'm all for these recounts. I agree with the thousands of out-of-state lawyers currently clogging every Holiday Inn in the state: We must discern the intent of EVERY VOTER. In fact, I think we should count people who had planned to vote, but, for whatever reason, never got around to actually go to the polls. I think we should count people who failed to register, but have a good excuse, such as they forgot. I think we should count people who live in less-dramatic states such as Delaware, but would have moved to Florida and registered if they had known how exciting this election was going to be.

Why should these people be disenfranchised? We can discern their intentions, with the help of out-of-state lawyers!

So I believe that recounts, in principle, are a swell idea. At least I did when they involved only Palm Beach and Broward counties. But I became VERY nervous when Miami-Dade County decided to recount its ballots. Because it appeared likely that the Miami-Dade recount would have been the deciding factor in the election. In other words — and if the following statement does not send a chill down your

31

spine, then you do not have a spine — *Miami-Dade would have chosen the next president.*

This would not be good for America. Because if there's one thing that Miami-Dade has proven, time and again, it is this: WE DON'T KNOW HOW TO COUNT. We're the county that cheerfully paid a contractor $400,000 too much for "royal" palm trees that were more like palm shrubs. (Although I still believe these trees should be allowed to vote.) We're also the county that paid more than $1 million for road-striping work that was not, if you want to get technical about it, done, in the sense of stripes physically appearing on a road.

And Miami is of course the city that elected a mayor (at least temporarily) with the help of votes cast by, among others, Manuel Yip, who, at the time of the election, turned out to have been deceased for four years.

My point is that, when it comes to keeping an accurate count of things — dollars, trees, live voters vs. dead voters, whatever — Miami-Dade has a poor track record. Not to mention the fact that our voters have probably done some REALLY weird things with their ballots. ("Hey, this one has some kind of white powder on it!" "Yeah? Well, THIS one has a bullet hole.")

So letting Miami-Dade recount its votes, and thus pick the next president, would have been not unlike turning the controls of a 747 over to a chimpanzee. There is no telling WHERE we'd wind up. There could be a BIG vote surge for Elián.

That's why, today, I am thankful. I'm thankful that Miami-Dade has — incredibly — done the sane thing, and decided to stay out of this mess.

The rest of the United States (which already wishes that Florida still belonged to Spain) can blame Palm Beach and Broward for whatever happens. For once, Miami-Dade won't be the Lunatic County. We should all be thankful for that, and today, when we prepare to carve our Thanksgiving turkey, we should pause to reflect on our good fortune, and to imagine — in the true spirit of Thanksgiving — that our turkey is an out-of-state lawyer.

Party Time, Texas-Style:
Even the Cows Had a Ball

WASHINGTON

Every four years, this stodgy city kicks off its wingtip shoes. Then it puts on shoes that are even less comfortable, and celebrates the inauguration of a president.

And so the federal government — as only the federal government knows how — has gone into Festivity Implementation and Facilitation Mode. Unfortunately, the weather was awful. But the rain, freezing temperatures, and occasional death from exposure have not put a damper on the inauguration and its upbeat theme: "We're Cold, and We're Wet."

No, seriously, the official theme, as far as I can tell, is: "We're Texans, and By God We're From Texas!" This place is infested with Texans, who simply cannot get over how Texan they are. Many of them are wearing cowboy hats, though I suspect they're mainly business people who have never personally interacted with a cow that was not in the form of prime rib.

So the new administration will definitely have a "Texas style," as opposed to the old administration, which had an "Arkansas style." The Washington news media have made a big deal out of this changeover, although in fact there is no discernible difference between the two styles, both of which basically consist of people going: "Whooo-EEE!"

Speaking of Arkansas style: Bill Clinton had a very classy final full day in office, didn't he? Mr. Legacy signed a deal with the special prosecutor in which he finally came clean and admitted, in no uncertain terms, that he — to quote from his statement — "may or may not have said things under oath that may or may not have been less than totally truthful, or possibly not, depending on how you define 'not.'" Mr. Clinton also admitted to "a possible involvement" in four convenience-store robberies. Of course, these blemishes on his record must be weighed against the many accomplishments of his administration, which, according to the estimated four hundred and fifty farewell speeches given by Mr. Clinton, include peace, prosperity, gravity, pasteurization, the plow, and Handel's *Messiah*.

But the focus now is on our new president, George W. Bush III Jr., who, along with his gracious wife, Mrs. George W. Bush III Jr., has been attending numerous inaugural balls, which are real Washington-style fun-a-paloozas.

I attended a hot-ticket ball hosted by the Texas State Society for nine thousand paying guests and several head of actual cattle. I am searching for a way to tell you how much fun this ball was. Okay, try this: Imagine that you're at a major airport on a Friday night, and all the flights have been canceled, so that thousands of travelers are jammed together in long, jostling, increasingly hostile lines for food, drink, bathrooms, escalators, everything. Now imagine that everybody is wearing formal clothes, and the atmosphere is 97 percent hairspray fumes, and every few seconds somebody, who always seems to be right next to your ear, shouts "Whooo-EEE!"

That's the kind of fun we were having. This ball was so crowded that it took me — a trained professional journalist with vast experience in this area — forty-five minutes to get a beer. I am fervently hoping that the highest domestic priority of the new administration will be: more bartenders. In between balls, they held the actual inauguration ceremony, featuring music by rap star Eminem.

No, seriously, it featured traditional patriotic tunes, played by the traditional band of military people armed with tubas. The ceremony was very dignified, except when Al Gore, understandably, lost control, and Barbara Bush had to coldcock him with the Bush family Bible. After that, George W. took the oath of office; he did this flawlessly, except for ending with the words "so help me, Rhonda." Then he read a nice speech in which he pointed out — correctly, in my view — that the future lies ahead. Then it was . . . back to the balls!

Call me corny, but seeing this in person — this orderly transfer of the greatest power on Earth — made me feel something that I have never felt before. I think it might be frostbite.

Next we have some columns I wrote from the 2000 Republican and Democratic national conventions. I have been to ten national political conventions, and I have yet to see a single important decision get made at one. Nothing important ever happens at these things: They're just an excuse to hold lavish parties where big corporations try to influence politicians and the media with free food and liquor. So I think they're great.

It's Party Time, As Philly
Gets Phunky

PHILADELPHIA

It's convention time, and Republicans from all over the solar system have gathered here in the historic birthplace of our nation — the place where in 1776, as any American schoolchild can tell you, the Founding Fathers signed the Gettysburg Address.

Very little has happened here since then. But that is about to change. We are in for a wild and wacky week, because the Republicans have declared that their convention theme this year will be "Get Phunky in Philly!" They are determined to shed their image as a stodgy, exclusive party for wealthy white conservative Mercedes-driving country-club members. This year, in the words of convention chairman Jim Nicholson, "We want to show the world that we also welcome people who drive certain models of Jaguar."

With that goal in mind, the Republican nominee, George "W." Bush Jr. III, went out of his way to select a running mate who would broaden the ticket, in the sense of not being a member of "W's" immediate family.

To help him narrow down the list of possibilities, Bush called on veteran political insider Dick "Dick" Cheney, who conducted an exhaustive, wide-ranging search that took him to every corner of his house before he finally settled on: himself.

And with good reason. Cheney has an impressive résumé: At various times in his career, he has served as secretary of defense, presidential chief of staff, congressperson, senior lifeguard, Wyoming state tango champion, and bass player for the Sex Pistols. He also is the perfect balance for the ticket, because whereas Bush is a wealthy white Yale-educated Protestant Western oil guy, Cheney is a wealthy white Yale-educated Protestant Western oil guy who is a *completely different age*. As Bush himself put it, in a press conference announcing the Cheney nomination, "I'm fifty-four years old, whereas Dick is fifty-nine, so that's a difference of eight years right there."

These two men will formally be nominated on Thursday night, but not before the Republicans subject the nation to many, many hours of Harmony.

They are anxious to avoid the hostile tone of previous GOP conventions, which usually featured Pat Buchanan setting fire to life-size mannequins representing the Supreme Court. This year will be different. This year the convention will feature a softer tone and, in the words of chairman Nicholson, "minorities out the wazooty." The focus will be positive: There will be no references to the scandals of the Clinton administration, other than Tuesday night's scheduled eighty-five-minute prime-time address by Monica Lewinsky.

Also, Bush has instituted a strict rule prohibiting convention speakers from making direct personal attacks on President Bill Clinton or his wife, Mrs. President Bill Clinton.

To enforce this rule, the Republicans will be using a special computerized "smart" podium programmed to deliver a powerful electric shock to any speaker who utters code words or phrases that could be construed as subtle attacks on the first couple, such as "liars" or "criminals" or "big-thighed golf-cheating intern-groping cigar pervert."

This podium was tested over the weekend by a courageous volunteer, the Rev. Pat Robertson, who somehow managed to survive, although he did lose all his body hair.

So if all goes according to plan, the Republicans' convention will be so smooth and glitch-free that even the actual speakers will have trouble staying awake.

But that does NOT mean there will be no excitement! For one thing, numerous protesters are on hand hoping to gain media attention and thus transmit to all of humanity the urgent message that they are wackos without jobs.

Also, the city of Philadelphia desperately hopes that it can use the convention coverage to showcase itself as a tourist destination where tourists would deliberately stop for some reason other than transmission trouble. There's lots to do here!

For example (I am not making this example up), Philadelphia's Official Delegate and Media Guide lists, under "attractions," both New Jersey AND Delaware.

So it's definitely going to be an exciting week of GOP-style fun. I'll be writing daily reports for you, bringing you all the action, both from inside the convention hall, and from the streets. I am assuming here that Delaware HAS streets.

Party Politics: Reporters Get Invited to Some, Crash Others

PHILADELPHIA

A critical function that we journalists perform at political conventions is to try to get into parties that we have not been invited to. There are dozens of these parties, sponsored by large corporations with a sincere public-spirited desire to become larger.

We journalists crash these parties so that we can bring you the "inside story" on what the political "bigwigs" are doing "behind the scenes." What they are doing, it always turns out, is standing around talking about what other parties they plan to go to. Nothing newsworthy ever happens. But we journalists keep trying to get in; we are like moths attracted to a street light, hurling their little moth bodies repeatedly against the glass, driven by a powerful natural instinct to obtain free corporate liquor.

Thus it was that I found myself standing on a rain-slicked Philadelphia sidewalk with a fellow journalist named Joel, trying to get into a "tribute" sponsored by Daimler-Chrysler Corp. for Rep. J. C. Watts, who is the most prominent African-American Republican in Congress, in the same sense that Ringo was the most prominent drummer in the Beatles.

This party featured entertainment by the Temptations. (Other entertainers at this convention include — I swear — Dick Clark, Chubby Checker, the Four Tops, the Shirelles, Bobby Vee, and Bo Derek; strict Republican bylaws prohibit appearances by any performer who has had any kind of hit since 1974.) Unfortunately, the security people would not let us in to see the Temptations, so we stood outside and watched the Republicans "jiving," as only Republicans can, to the smooth sounds of the great Motown group, whose dance steps were as dazzling as ever, even with the use of walkers. Although I was not admitted, I enjoyed myself, and I feel no bitterness toward Daimler-Chrysler Corp., whose cars explode on contact with shopping carts.

Things perked up when Joel and I latched on to Robert Novak, a conservative pundit with a tan like a traffic cone. He was walking to a party being thrown for him and some other CNN people by a company called "Sallie Mae." In Republican circles, Novak is Elvis: People were calling out his name and applauding him as he strode along. At one point, I swear, an extremely excited man sprinted half a block to catch Novak and breathlessly report that he was going to run for Congress against Dick Gephardt.

"Great," said Novak, still walking.

"The early polls look very good!" said the man. He appeared to be on the verge of wetting his pants.

"Great," said Novak, not slowing down.

"This is breaking news, Bob!" shouted the man to Novak's back as Novak strode rapidly away, his tan radiating into the damp Philadelphia evening.

Because Joel and I had latched on, lamprey-like, to one of the honorees, we got into the party, which was jammed with people talking about what parties they were going to next. Among the luminaries on hand was billionaire Steve Case, who started America Online. I tried to start a conversation with him, but I kept getting cut off. (Rim shot.)

But seriously, it was a fine party, in the

sense that there was free beer. I want everybody reading this column to find out what "Sallie Mae" makes and go buy some of it.

I'm out of space, so here are the headlines:

CONVENTION UPDATE: The convention has started, and formally declared itself to be in favor of children.

"DICK" CHENEY UPDATE: The Democrats, moving fast, have already released a TV commercial linking Dick to the JFK assassination.

GEORGE "W." BUSH JR. III UPDATE: He is, I swear, in Ohio. Somebody better get him a map.

PROTESTER UPDATE: It turns out that the United States is run by corrupt corporate fascist pigs. I'll try to find out more by infiltrating their parties.

"Rolling Roll Call" Makes Bad Idea Last Even Longer

PHILADELPHIA

Now HERE'S a great idea from the Republicans.

You know the roll-call votes they take at conventions? I'm talking about when the state delegation chairpersons get up, one by one, and — before revealing how their states are going to vote, which everybody already knows — drone on about how great their states are, even if the state is a known armpit:

"Mr. Chairman, the great state of Alabama, proud home of the largest Methodist-owned ottoman reupholstering plant east of the Mississippi; birthplace of the steam-powered pig castrator; site of the world's tallest free-standing pile of used truck tires; consistently rated among the top five states in the nation for spittoon safety; the state whose official state university proudly owns a complete set of the 1979 *Encyclopedia Britannica* except for volume IV (Dachshund–Easter Island), which whoever has it should please return it immediately; the state with more Big Boy restaurants per capita than. . . ."

. . . and so on, state by state, until every TV viewer in America has switched over to watching reruns of *Gilligan's Island.* Except for big stupid hats shaped like elephants or donkeys, these roll calls are the single most-ridiculed element of political conventions. Everybody agrees that they are boring, moronic, and spectacularly inefficient.

And so guess what the Republicans have done? They have come up with a New Idea! The party of Change, the party of Efficiency, the Party of Getting Things Done, has figured out a way to make the roll call last for THREE NIGHTS.

Yes. They're calling it a "rolling roll call," and the way it works is, they do only a third of the states each night, except that some of the states, after bragging for ten minutes about their achievements (". . . birthplace of fat-free canoe wax . . .") declare that they are PASSING, which means the next night they vote AGAIN. At this rate, the Republicans may never get

48

around to actually nominating George "W." Bush III Jr., which means they'll be legally forced to recycle Viagra spokesperson Bob Dole, who, when asked about this possibility, declared, "I'm up for it!" (Rim shot.)

So most of the action here is taking place on the streets, where protesters continue to fight for Meaningful Change via the highly effective technique of shouting semi-coherent slogans at police officers, police horses, and small, baffled clots of civilians. I watched one protest march, which consisted of about 1,000 people representing, at a conservative estimate, 7,000 different causes. Here is just a partial list of the things that the protesters were angry about: war, poverty, hunger, racism, homelessness, disease, pollution, police brutality, the death penalty, the judicial system, the anti-missile defense system, the System, animal abuse, corporations, sweatshops, authority, rich people, money in general, stadium construction, the Republican Party, the Democratic Party, the federal government, meat, and, of course, The Gap.

To dramatize these causes, some protesters had dressed themselves as giant cockroaches; others were wearing cardboard mouse heads; and others were carrying (Why not?) large cardboard peanuts. One man was brandishing a four-foot-long toothbrush and, through an electric bullhorn, shouting "LET ELVIS BE PRESIDENT! WHY IN THE WORLD CAN'T A DEAD MAN BE PRESIDENT?!?" To be fair, this man may have been just fooling around, unlike the serious protesters wearing the cockroach costumes.

Here's the rest of the convention news:

"DICK" CHENEY UPDATE: The Democratic Party has released another attack ad, this one charging that, while he was a congressman in Wyoming, Cheney had an "unusually close friendship" with a sheep named Bernice. Cheney immediately issued an angry denial, stating that it was "strictly platonic" and "her name was Jennifer."

PARTY UPDATE: Greed-crazed fascist corporate pigs continue to try to corrupt the political process by holding lavish parties wherein they try to bribe politicians and the media with free food and liquor. I say we give them whatever they want.

Encounter with Falwell
Gets Surprisingly Intimate

PHILADELPHIA

I'll fill you in on the other exciting convention developments in a moment, but first I want to talk frankly and openly about my relationship with the Extremely Rev. Jerry Falwell. I want to get this thing "out in the open," before the gossip-mongers start with their rumor and innuendo. Because Reverend Falwell and I have done *nothing to be ashamed of.*

Here's how it happened: On Tuesday night, Reverend Falwell and I were guests in back-to-back segments on MSNBC, which is broadcasting the convention live to a nationwide audience consisting of Mr. and Mrs. Herbert A. Pocklewinger of Sioux Falls, South Dakota. We were interviewed by Tom Brokaw and Tim Russert, who sit high above the convention floor in a glass booth staffed by men with cattle prods, which are used to jolt Tom and Tim awake when the commercials end.

Reverend Falwell was on the show to talk about gay people, whom, as a Christian, he sincerely and deeply loves, which is why he wants to inform them that they are degenerate perverts going to hell. I have no earthly idea why I was on the show. All I know is that, when Reverend Falwell was done with his segment, a technician removed the earpiece from his ear, and — with the reverend standing right next to me, our hips practically touching — the technician inserted the SAME EAR-PIECE, which was still warm, into MY ear.

Yes, there was penetration. Yes, there was probably an exchange of earwax. No, neither I nor Reverend Falwell (as far as I know) was wearing a condom. But so what? This is the year 2000, darn it! If two consenting male adults choose to share an earpiece, it is nobody else's business! That is my view, and I'm sure the reverend agrees, although I have not discussed this with him personally. (Jerry, if you're reading this, call me, you big lug!)

Meanwhile, on the social front, the Republicans continue to "get down," GOP-style. I attended a totally "happening" outdoor party called (I swear) IRA-PALOOZA. It was sponsored by Merrill Lynch, Morgan Stanley Dean Witter, and other large, fun-loving financial corporations to celebrate the passage of something called "HR 1102," which has something to do with Individual Retirement Accounts, and which I totally support, because there was free liquor.

Party-wise, IRA-PALOOZA was identical to its namesake, the Lollapalooza rock festival, except that instead of rock acts blasting heavy metal, there was a wedding-reception-style band quietly tooting the greatest hits of 1937, and instead of half-naked young people writhing ecstatically in a mosh pit, there were Republicans in dark suits networking on cellphones. Some of them were using earpieces, but I stayed faithful to Jerry.

After about ninety fun-filled seconds at IRA-PALOOZA, I tore myself away. A few blocks away, I found myself in the middle of the daily street protest, in which protesters, the overwhelming majority of whom appear to be middle-class white kids, demonstrate their solidarity with The People by running around shouting and blocking streets, thereby inconveniencing the actual people of Philadelphia. At one point, I watched some protesters, wearing bandannas to protect their Secret Identities, drag some newspaper boxes into the street, blocking it. This infuriated a woman waiting at a bus stop.

"What's WRONG with you people?" she shouted. "I want to go HOME!"

Crying, she started dragging the boxes off the street, so her bus could come through. The protesters ran on, some yelling, "THESE ARE OUR STREETS! F— THE REPUBLICANS!" I couldn't figure out why, if they hate the Republicans so much, they didn't just go over and hassle IRA-PALOOZA, instead of working people. But what do I know? I'm just a corporate-media whore. Speaking of which, my ear feels funny.

George W. Survives His GOP Convention Speech

PHILADELPHIA

The Republicans finally ran out of minority groups, so on Thursday night they had no choice but to listen to the actual nominee, George "W." Bush III Jr. IV, who gave an acceptance speech that was pretty much flawless, except for the eight times he referred to the United States as "Venezuela."

Then the convention — which lasted four days, or, if you were actually here, seventeen months — came to a dramatic climax, as more than four thousand Republican delegates and alternates joined together and, in a striking display of party harmony, beat James Carville to death.

No, seriously, the Republicans were Positive and Harmonious right to the end, celebrating and "getting down" as only Republicans can. NOBODY dances like Republican convention delegates.

When the band starts playing a "rock 'n' roll" tune, they sense that they should respond somehow, even though generations of selective GOP breeding have eliminated all traces of rhythm from their genetic makeup. Gamely, they lurch up and down at random, like the moles in a Whack-a-Mole arcade game, thrusting their BUSH-CHENEY signs into the air. The Republican Delegate Boogie!

Which is not to say the convention was no fun. There were many fine parties, sponsored by many fine corporations that should, in my opinion, be allowed to do whatever the hell they want.

The highlight for me came at a lavish corporate party for the movie industry at an exclusive nightclub. I went there with five cartoonists; we got in basically by whining. Inside, there was a VIP area, guarded by security men the size of UPS trucks, reserved for important guests, which definitely did not include us.

So we made our own VIP area. In the middle of a largish room, there was a platform the size of a Ping-Pong table, raised about a foot off the floor. We climbed onto it, and we put an orange traffic cone on the edge to indicate that it was an exclusive area. For the first half-hour, it was just the six of us up there. People would walk into the room, and we'd shout, "Sorry! VIP area! You can't come up here!" And they'd stride briskly away, avoiding eye contact with us.

But then an amazing thing happened: An actual VIP joined us! It was Dick Armey, the majority leader of the House of Representatives. I am not making this up. I'm still not sure why Representative Armey got up there with us; perhaps he had consumed some refreshing beverages. But he was friendly, and he stayed for quite a while, and he told us a pretty funny joke that I will not repeat here except to say that it involved a naughty interpretation of the phrase "Dick Armey."

And guess what? Once word got around the party that Dick had been in our VIP area, more VIPs started showing up! Pretty soon we were joined by Jack Valenti, head of the Motion Picture Association of America and by so many Republican elected officials that we had to start kicking them off the platform. And if you don't think it's pretty darned funny to watch a cartoonist order a member of Congress off a small, crowded platform, then you have not consumed as much beer as I did.

So it was a fun week, but now it's time for the Republicans to pack their bags and go home and untie their servants. For us in the media, it's on to Los Angeles and the Democratic convention. A whole week of Al Gore Mania! I can't wait! Maybe my plane will crash.

Real People, Real Issues, Full Nudity

LOS ANGELES

Thousands of Democratic delegates have gathered here this week with one purpose in mind: to get to the convention center from their hotels, some of which are as far away as Oregon. In the unlikely event that they succeed, they plan to nominate Al Gore, who is running for president on the campaign slogan "Al Gore: He Was Not Legally Involved in the Clinton Administration."

The slogan is designed to subtly suggest that Gore had nothing to do with the various administration scandals, and never personally visited the White House. Gore reinforced this theme by boldly selecting, as his vice presidential running mate, Connecticut senator Joseph Lieberman, who makes history by being the first person ever on a major-party ticket whose name can be rearranged to spell "I JAB

HERPES MELON."

Choosing Lieberman was a shrewd strategic move, intended to broaden the appeal of the Democratic ticket. Lieberman is known as a moral, pro-family-values senator who is more conservative than Gore on many issues and who, in fact, announced on Friday that he intends to vote for the Republican ticket.

"As moral and conservative as I am," he said, "I just can't see me voting for us."

The Republicans moved swiftly to counter Gore's selection. On Sunday morning, the Republican nominee, George "W." Bush III Jr., told Tim Russert of NBC News that, in his opinion, Dick Cheney is Jewish.

So the tactical maneuvering has started, and it looks like an exciting campaign ahead, with most polls now showing Gore-Lieberman closing to within just two percentage points of Bush-Cheney among the estimated four voters who currently care.

But for this week, the spotlight will be on the Democrats, who are determined that their convention will draw more TV viewers than the tightly scripted, rigidly controlled show put on by the Republicans. In the words of Terry McAuliffe, chairman of the Democratic National

Convention Committee: "We're going to show real Americans talking about real issues. And there will be full frontal nudity."

Speaking of which: The highlight speakers of the first night of the convention will be President Bill Clinton and his wife, New York resident Mrs. President Bill Clinton. The president will speak last, delivering what is expected to be an emotional look back at the highlights of his presidency, culminating in a standing ovation as giant overhead nets open up and drop thousands of pairs of red-white-and-blue thong underwear on the cheering delegates.

But much of the "real action" at this convention will take place outside the convention hall, in the dazzling, glamorous city of Los Angeles, whose magnificent mansions, swank restaurants, and star-studded population certainly justify its nickname, "The Big Apple." The Democrats will be holding many lavish, exclusive fundraisers this week, raising the millions and millions of dollars they will need to carry out the vital work of producing TV commercials that portray the Republicans as the party of the rich.

I have rented a car and will be "on the

scene" here, reporting all the news to you, just as soon as I figure out the freeway system. So you'll never hear from me again.

There's Glitz, Glamour,
the Clintons — but Where's Al?

LOS ANGELES

The Democrats are really fired up, especially after President Clinton's stirring speech Monday night, in which he told the cheering delegates that he may be eligible to serve a third term, "depending on your definition of what the Constitution means by the word 'no.' "

The president and the first lady, Mrs. President Bill Clinton, also attended many lavish star-studded fundraising events, where they raised millions of dollars for two favorite causes: (1) The Bill Clinton Presidential Library and Hot Tub, and (2) The Committee to Elect Hillary Senator from New York or, If That Doesn't Work Out, Maybe Illinois.

Meanwhile, Al Gore was in — I am not making this up — Cleveland. Rumor has it that the Gore camp is ticked off at the

Clintons for hogging all the money and famous movie stars before Al gets here, as evidenced by the fact that Al's lone scheduled fundraising event is a "Cruller-a-Rama" at a Dunkin' Donuts in Burbank, which will be celebrity-hosted, according to the Gore campaign press release, by "Ricardo Montalban, unless he is already dead."

Speaking of excitement: The protesters are here, delivering the same persuasive message that they delivered at the Republican convention: "Hey! Look at us!" I went to watch them protest in Santa Monica, which is maybe five miles from my hotel as the crow flies, or roughly 857 miles on the convenient Southern California freeway system.

Unfortunately, I was following directions given orally to me by my friend Chip Bok, who is a professional cartoonist and therefore not familiar with words. As I understood his directions, at pretty much every intersection I came to I was supposed to turn right. At one point I called Chip to say I was lost, and we had this conversation:

CHIP: Can you see the ocean?

ME: I think so.

CHIP: Well, it's right near there.

I eventually found the protest, which consisted of protesters videotaping each other and shouting "SELLOUT!" at Democrats going to a party inside an amusement park on the Santa Monica Pier, sponsored by various large, greedy fascist corporations. Holding the protesters back were police officers on large horses, which are very effective because you know that they will not hesitate to step and/or poop on you, regardless of your constitutional right to protest. "Constitution, Schmonstitution," that is the feeling of police horses.

Many of the Democrats going into the party seemed chagrined about being called corporate lackey scum — as if they were Republicans or something! Probably some of them used to be long-haired, hippie-style protesters themselves, standing on the other side of the police horses, shouting at the Fat Cats. And now they were accused of BEING the Fat Cats!

Not that this kept them from going inside to snork down free corporate fascist food and drink. As a dedicated journalist, I also went into the amusement park; the highlight for me was the bumper cars, which are kind of like the freeway system, except more efficient. At one point, I saw one of the Democratic guests, a middle-aged man, driving a bumper car *while talking on his cellphone*. It's time for the Revolution.

Campaign Trail, Freeways, Finally Lead to a Vast Parking Lot

LOS ANGELES

I'm in a taxi, somewhere in Los Angeles. Or it could be Oklahoma. We just passed, I swear, some oil rigs.

I'm trying to get to the Democratic convention. I gave up on the official shuttle-bus system, which apparently was designed by the same person who decided how many lifeboats there should be on the *Titanic*. So now I'm in a taxi on — Surprise! — a freeway. Under strict California law, you cannot go anywhere, including the bathroom, without going on at least three freeways, two of which must be the "10" and the "405."

After a few hundred miles we arrive at the Staples Center, which is named for the giant office-supplies chain Office Max. To give the Staples Center a friendly, laid-back California "vibe," the city has accessorized it with barricades, razor-wire fences, police dogs, police horses, and hundreds of police officers with large police biceps from lifting weights and dropping them on the heads of alleged perpetrators resisting arrest. They're polite and professional, but it's hard not to be a little nervous around them; you can't help but remember that shocking videotape a few years back, showing a group of LAPD horses beating up on Rodney King's horse.

Outside the perimeter fence, baking in the heat, is a vast parking lot that has been designated as the Protest Area, because it would be rude to call it the Raving Loon Area. Up on the stage, bellowing into a microphone, is a man wearing (Why not?) a hard hat with a huge flip-down sun visor, flipped up. He is bellowing about God. Listening to him are a total of two pro-God people, and maybe a dozen bored, heckling protesters, who are waiting for Democratic delegates to arrive so they can call them fascist corporate sellouts. These listeners are all within twenty-five feet of the speaker; he could easily talk to them in an unamplified voice. But he chooses to bellow at them via the huge, stadium-quality public-address system. It's like using an army tank to crack a walnut.

"THERE IS ONE GOD!" he bellows.

"No!" shouts a protester. "Two!"

"That's right!" shouts another. "Two gods!"

The speaker informs them that they will go to hell (presumably via the "10" and the "405"). He then asks if there are any questions.

"Yes!" shouts somebody. "Where did you get your hat?"

"YOU CAN GET IT AT A SAFETY-SUPPLY STORE!" bellows the speaker.

As I walk away, the speaker and the protesters are arguing about the Third World.

"THE THIRD WORLD DOESN'T KNOW WHAT TOILET PAPER IS!" bellows the speaker, his words echoing across the parking lot. "THEY DON'T KNOW WHAT A TOILET IS!"

"You're a toilet!" shouts a protester.

And so it continues, the vital ideological struggle for control of the Protest Area.

Meanwhile, in the convention hall, Democrats, at least the ones who got buses, have boldly come out in favor of both prosperity AND children. They put these positions right in their platform, which places them in stark contrast with the Republicans, whose platform calls for worldwide depression and the shooting of children for sport. Both parties' platforms will, in accordance with tradition, be buried in a landfill in New Jersey and never surface.

In other political news, we have these updates on the Democratic ticket:

- AL GORE UPDATE: Al is practicing for his big speech, which according to one of his aides will feature "several near-human hand gestures."
- JOSEPH LIEBERMAN UPDATE: Senator Lieberman, who has been critical of Hollywood's lax morals, apparently has softened his stance after a nine-hour meeting in a luxury hotel suite with the cast of *Sex and the City*. "This issue is WAAAAAAAY more complex than I thought," he told the *Los Angeles Times*, moments before passing out.

Joe Goes Hollywood As
Al Plans to Be "Riveting"

LOS ANGELES

In a surprise development Wednesday night, vice presidential nominee Joseph Lieberman, continuing to soften his previously harsh stance on Hollywood morals, delivered his entire acceptance speech without pants.

"I love this crazy town!" he told the delegates, adding: "Jennifer Lopez, please call me back!"

But the real highlight of the convention is expected to come at the grand finale tonight, which promises to deliver all of the drama, passion, and high-voltage excitement conjured up by the words "Al Gore."

According to a source in the Gore camp, the vice president has prepared a "riveting" speech, featuring some "challenging views" on how the America of the Twenty-first Century "can recycle a larger percentage of its mulch." During the speech, which is expected to draw a nationwide television audience of Tim Russert, Los Angeles riot police will surround the convention hall to prevent delegates from escaping.

Speaking of security: A group of cartoonists and I have discovered an excellent way to get into lavish parties that we are not invited to, which is the main function of journalists at political conventions. Our secret is that we made friends with the mayor of Los Angeles, Richard "Dick" Riordan. I am not making this up.

We met Mayor Dick for breakfast at a restaurant he owns in downtown Los Angeles called the Pantry, which produces an estimated two-thirds of the world's cholesterol. Mayor Dick is a plain-spoken type of person who enjoys a good joke and would not mind seeing the *Los Angeles Times* destroyed with tactical nuclear weapons. During breakfast, he told us that he was going to a party that night, and we asked if we could be his security detail, and he said sure.

So at 9 P.M., seven of us met at the party site, dressed as security personnel. We wore dark suits and sunglasses, and each of us had a cord plugged into his ear. These were coiled cords, taken from our hotel telephones, so you can imagine how professional we looked.

For security purposes, we gave ourselves code names. Mine was "Magenta Eagle." The others were: "T and T," "Kitchen Magician," "Thrusting Rod," "Booger," "Pocket Fisherman," and "Eggplant."

We stood in a small professional bunch in the parking lot, discussing security-related matters ("What's my code name again?") and surveying the crowd of arriving party guests, which was not easy because it was dark and we were wearing sunglasses. Finally we located Mayor Dick (code name: "Sourdough") and his wife ("Pork Chop").

We surrounded them in a standard clot formation and approached the party entrance, talking in code into our hotel phone cords. They let us all walk right in.

As dedicated professionals, we continued to provide vigilant security for the mayor and his wife all the way to the bar, at which point they were on their own.

I would say the highlight of the evening came about a half-hour later, when it was time for the mayor and his wife to leave for another party, and she said, quote, "Sourdough! Sourdough! We have to go!"

The low point came when one of our agents, Pocket Fisherman ("Chip Bok"), found that he had inserted his phone cord so far into his ear that he couldn't get it out.

And people think journalism is easy.

Now It's Safe to Do Some Unconventional Thinking

LOS ANGELES

The Democratic convention ended on a high note Thursday night as Al Gore accepted the nomination with a speech that really "rocked the house," especially the unscripted, totally spontaneous moment when he called Tipper onto the podium to help demonstrate a new organic composting technique.

Al's moment of triumph was tarnished only slightly when his running mate, Sen. Joe Lieberman — continuing to soften his criticism of entertainment-industry morals — announced that he is quitting the Democratic ticket to get hair plugs and take a role in the forthcoming movie *Porky's XI*.

"It's a part that I feel will help me grow, as an actor," he told the *Washington Post*, adding, "I play a girls' gym teacher."

So there is no question that Gore,

already trailing in the polls, faces an uphill fight. But the polls are not everything. Remember that in 1984, Walter Mondale was also trailing in the polls, and he went on to defeat Ronald Reagan in several parts of Minnesota.

So nobody really knows what will happen this year when the American voters — who so far have been snoozing through the presidential race — wake up, take a hard look at the candidates, and fall back asleep.

For now, though, the important thing is that the conventions are finally over. Once again, you can safely click through the TV channels without running the risk that the screen will suddenly be filled with the face of James Carville, permanently traumatizing your children.

So this is a good time for us to reflect on the American political-convention system, and ask ourselves what we could do to make it less stupid.

Here are my suggestions:

1. ELIMINATE THE DELEGATES. I frankly have no idea why these people attend. They make no decisions other than whether to wave their signs up-and-down or side-to-side (somebody else decides what the signs actually SAY). They also

clog up the hotel lobbies and consume vital taxi resources needed by professional journalists trying to get to corporate-sponsored parties.

2. HAVE ANTI-CLICHÉ RULES FOR CONVENTION SPEAKERS. For example, if a speaker began a speech by saying, "As I stand before you . . ." or if at any point in his speech he mentioned "the Twenty-first Century," a trapdoor in the podium would open and the speaker would drop like a bag of cement, never to be seen again. A strictly enforced anti-cliché policy could cut the total combined speech time for an entire convention to under fifteen minutes.

3. HOLD THE CONVENTIONS IN LAS VEGAS. Picture this: It's prime time on the final night, and the nominee is scheduled to make his acceptance speech. The convention hall is rocking, the networks are broadcasting the scene live, but . . . the nominee isn't there! Because . . . he's winning at the craps table! Wouldn't that be GREAT?

4. CREATE SOME KIND OF FEDERAL AFFIRMATIVE-ACTION PROGRAM TO SUPPLY CELEBRITIES TO THE REPUBLICANS. All they have now is Bo Derek. The Republicans

dragged that poor woman to EVERY-THING; it will take her several face-lifts to fully recover. Meanwhile, at the Democratic convention, you couldn't open a car door without hitting, at minimum, Jimmy Smits.

5. REQUIRE PROTESTERS TO BE ABLE TO GIVE A CLEAR EXPLANATION OF WHY THEY ARE PROTESTING THAT DOES NOT INVOLVE SHOUTING AN INCOHERENT SLOGAN ABOUT "THE PEOPLE," WHICH THEY LEARNED ON THE INTERNET.

So yes, the system could be better. But it's still pretty darned good. And although I have "poked some fun" at both the Democrats and the Republicans over the past few weeks, I think it's important for us all to remember, as American voters, that BOTH major parties, whatever their faults, think we're morons. So don't forget to vote!

And Joe Lieberman, if you're reading this, please call your agent.

Next we have some columns that I wrote while covering the Winter Olympics in Salt Lake City, Utah, in 2002. I love the Olympics, because they enable people from all over the world to come together and — regardless of their political or cultural differences — accuse each other of cheating.

Call Security:
The Torch Is on Fire!

SOMEWHERE IN UTAH

The mood is very festive here, as tens of thousands of fun-loving people have gathered for the Winter Olympics, along with an equal number of fun-loving, bomb-sniffing dogs.

Yes, security is tight here, which is why I cannot tell you exactly where "here" is, lest the terrorists find out about it. All I can reveal at this time is that we are in a city next to a large, salty lake. At least they *claim* it's salty. For security reasons, they are not letting anybody taste it.

The intense security has already caused an unfortunate incident involving the Olympic torch, which, after being painstakingly carried more than 10,000 miles from Athens, Greece, was extinguished upon crossing the Utah state line by suspicious security personnel, who noticed that it was — and this is a direct quote — "on fire." Also, it did not have a photo ID. Fortunately, this misunderstanding was straightened out, and the torch is expected to be released any day now from its cell at the Guantánamo Naval Base.

But such minor "snafus" will in no way put a damper on these Olympic Games, which are very important to Utah, whose residents hope to use the international spotlight to show the world that there is more to their state than just Donny and Marie Osmond. In the words of Utah governor Michael O. Leavitt, "There was also little Jimmy Osmond, and the older brothers . . . let's see . . . Jay? Billy? Wait, it'll come to me."

Utah was chosen to host these games by the International Olympic Committee after carefully weighing numerous wads of cash supplied by local organizers. But as far as I'm concerned, the bribery scandal is "ancient history," and I do not plan to mention it again, unless I can think of more jokes about it.

Besides, these Olympics are not about scandals. These Olympics are about answering a burning question, a question that has been asked for as long as there have been athletes competing in sports:

Will the press corps be able to obtain alcohol?

This question arises because Utah is the headquarters of a large religious organization that, out of respect for its privacy, I will refer to as "The Episcopal Church" (not its real name). Even though the Episcopal Church pretty much runs Utah, it's trying to keep a low profile during the Olympics. This is kind of like Godzilla trying to keep a low profile in Tokyo, but I'm not going to argue.

Anyway, the Episcopalians do not approve of alcohol, so it is not that easy to obtain here. Ironically, heroin is sold openly at convenience stores.

No, seriously, the Episcopalians also do not approve of drugs, caffeine, spicy food, or the party game "Twister."

This strict atmosphere has the international press corps alarmed. The international press corps did not come all the way to the Winter Olympics to watch the biathlon sober.

Needless to say, I will be delving deeply into this issue over the next two weeks, and reporting my findings to you. Time permitting, I will also report on sporting events, if I can get into any.

And of course I'll be reporting on life in

this exciting city, while being careful not to reveal its exact location. Because then I would have to kill you.

Frozen Lips, Barefoot Skaters — and Who Let All Those Dogs Out?

SALT LAKE CITY (DON'T TELL ANYBODY!)

The Winter Olympics got under way Friday night with a spectacular and very cold opening ceremony featuring some of the world's top entertainment artists, including country artist LeAnn Rimes, R&B artist R. Kelly, pop artist Sting, hip-hop artist Yo "Yo" Ma, and art artist Vincent van Gogh. These artists wowed the crowd by almost perfectly synchronizing their lip movements with recordings of themselves, although at one point Miss Rimes's lip gloss froze and bonded her mouth shut, forcing her to finish lip-syncing her song via hand puppet.

The only other glitch came when a technical foul-up forced the Mormon Tabernacle Choir, which was supposed to perform a medley of inspirational songs, to instead lip-sync "Who Let the Dogs Out?" But they pulled it off beautifully, because that is the kind of tabernacle artists they are.

The Opening Ceremony also featured a huge ice rink, on which eight hundred ice skaters did a synchronized routine that was hindered only slightly by the fact that they had to perform barefoot, because their skates could not go through the metal detector. The added security was necessary because the ceremony was attended by President Bush, or somebody who looks a lot like him. Vice President Dick Cheney also made a brief appearance in the form of a hologram.

Without question the most spectacular moment was the lighting of the Olympic flame. As usual, the details were kept "top secret" until the last minute, when the Olympic torch entered the stadium and, in a dramatic climax that brought a roar of approval from the crowd, ignited a twenty-five-foot-high stack of Enron executives.

But the most meaningful (in the sense of longest) part of the ceremony was the Parade of Athletes, in which competitors from many nations marched around the stadium and stood together, reminding us that the true meaning of the Olympics is international understanding, which means not making fun of foreign people because they have funny names. Among the Olympic athletes whose names we should not find amusing are (I am not making these up): Momo Skokic, Assen Pandov, Angel Pumpalov, Radek Bonk, Meelis Aasmae, Marku Uusipaavalniemi, Dagny L. Krisjandottir, Gatis Guts, Ganbat Jargalanchuluun, Frode Estil, Irina Slutskaya, Peter Pen, Beat Hefti, Miroslav Satan, Assol Slivets, and, of course, Picabo Street.

Speaking of which, the streets of Salt Lake City are teeming with helpful Olympic volunteers, who constantly ask you if they can help you, and then, whatever you want to do, helpfully inform you that, for security reasons, you cannot do it.

On a more positive note, it turns out that, contrary to the rumors, you can get beer here. All you have to do is ask. And then take a simple blood test. Then you must fight the giant snake.

No, really, it's no big deal to get a beer. Unfortunately, because of strict Utah laws, the beer has roughly the same alcohol content as Yoo-Hoo. The press corps is finding that it must consume massive quantities before it is prepared to face the biathlon competition.

I mention this not for personal reasons, but because I believe that it will be of widespread general interest to whoever reviews my expense account.

But never mind the finances. The important thing is, the games have begun. Soon the mountains will echo with the traditional Olympic cheer:

"Radek Bonk, he's our man!

"If he can't do it, Ganbat Jargalanchuluun can!"

For a Weird Cult,
They're Pretty Friendly

SALT LAKE MAXIMUM
SECURITY COMPOUND

Any day now, I promise to report on an actual Olympic sporting event. But first I want to tell you more about this fascinating place called Utah, which is nicknamed "The Beehive State," and for a very good reason: All the other nicknames were taken.

The main thing I've noticed is that most people here act very friendly. They even act friendly toward the news media, despite the fact they suspect (correctly) that WE suspect that they are members of a huge weird religious cult featuring multiple wives and secret underwear. We suspect this because downtown Salt Lake City is dominated by giant mysterious Mormon buildings that we're not allowed to enter. Naturally, we wonder what's going on in there. Human sacrifice?

Nude Jell-O wrestling?

TRUE FACT: Utah leads the nation in per capita Jell-O consumption.

The thing is, all religions seem weird if you're not familiar with them. For example, as a child in Armonk, New York, I attended St. Stephen's Episcopal Church, which had an unusual tradition, which I am not making up: On Easter Sunday, every member of the congregation was given a potted hyacinth, and then we'd sing a song with a lot of "alleluias" in it, and on every single alleluia, we'd all raise our hyacinths over our heads. If Mormons had walked in while this was going on, they'd have naturally assumed that we were a bunch of flower-worshiping wackos getting ready for some kind of bizarre cross-pollination ritual.

So, far be it for me to make fun of anybody's religion. But I will admit I was concerned because of stories I'd heard about aggressive Mormon proselytizing. I was afraid that I'd be walking past one of the giant Mormon buildings when — WHOA — a sidewalk trapdoor would open and I'd fall into a secret basement proselytizing dungeon equipped with torture instruments and (even worse) lime Jell-O.

But nothing like that has happened. In

fact, the only person who has approached me in a remotely proselytizing manner on the streets of Salt Lake City was a man named Yan Sun, who's with Falun Gong, a Chinese spiritual group that's being persecuted by the government of China. I know this because Yan Sun attached himself to me, barnacle-like, and stayed with me for five blocks, talking relentlessly, and the only way I could make him go away was by promising to write about his cause. So here goes:

HEY CHINA! LAY OFF FALUN GONG! OR ELSE!

Also on the streets of Salt Lake City, I saw a person striding along wearing a moose costume. I have no idea why. This could be a Mormon thing.

One final Utah mystery: In a shopping mall here, I saw an escalator with signs reading "CAUTION: PASSENGERS ONLY."

EARLY OLYMPIC COMPETITION RESULT: In a major upset, Grzjkystan defeated heavily favored Zrbykjstan in the finals of the men's eight-meter snowball fight.

SECURITY UPDATE: In what has been termed "an unfortunate mishap," a Norwegian ski jumper exceeded the prescribed altitude and was shot down by an F-15.

Competitive Ski Jumping
Is a Weighty Issue

PARK CITY, UTAH

I came here to watch the men's 90-meter ski jump, which gets its name from the fact that a sane person would have to drink a 90-meter-high glass of gin before he would even consider attempting this sport.

Of course, ski jumping was not invented by sane people. It was invented by Norwegians. These are people who eat a dish called "lutefisk," which can be either an entrée or an industrial solvent. So they think nothing of flinging themselves off cliffs.

If you've ever watched ski jumping on television, you've probably asked yourself: How do they DO that? How is it POSSIBLE? The answer to that question is two words — two words that define the spirit and essence of this amazing sport. Those words are: computer graphics. The "jumpers" are actually suspended by cables about a foot off the ground in a studio in Los Angeles. Also "Bob Costas" is an elaborate puppet operated by four people.

No, I'm kidding. I personally watched the ski jumpers here hurtle down an incredibly steep ramp, launch themselves off the end, soar through space long enough to qualify for beverage-cart service, then somehow land on their skis and slide, triumphantly, to the underwear-changing station. After each jump, two enthusiastic dudes would get on the public-address system and analyze it for the crowd. Most events at these Olympics have enthusiastic announcer dudes who are really, really into the sport, and thus are able to explain it in terms that only they understand. At ski jumping, they were always saying helpful things like: "Wow! He got a real huge float off his V!"

The 90-meter ski jump was won by — and in my opinion, this is a growing scandal here — three foreign persons. At a press conference afterward, one of them, Sven Hannawald of Germany, was asked if he could explain ski jumping to people who've never done it. Through an inter- preter, he answered: "If everybody tried, they would probably need very good insurance."

Also, to be competitive, they would need to lose weight. The big scandal in ski jumping is that a lot of the athletes have eating disorders, because the lighter you are, the farther you fly. There's talk of changing the rules to eliminate this advantage, possibly by requiring lighter competitors to carry extra weight. This concept is being studied in a series of experiments in which scientists are putting skis on former top Enron executives, tying anvils to their necks, and shoving them down the jump ramp.

"The early results are very promising," report the scientists. "These guys are getting practically no float off their V."

As a winter sports enthusiast, I urge these scientists to continue this important research, and if possible expand it to include the comedian Carrot Top.

OLYMPIC COMPETITION UPDATE: Turkey has won its first Winter Olympic gold ever in the Two-Man Windshield Scrape.

UTAH CULTURAL UPDATE: There is an establishment in Salt Lake City called the "Ho Ho Gourmet Restaurant."

Gosh! Heck! Utahans Angry About Skating

SALT LAKE CITY

People out here are so mad they could spit, if spitting were legal in Utah.

They're mad over this figure-skating scandal, which has the figure-skating world in such a state of confusion that National Guard troops have been called in to safeguard the mascara supply.

In case you don't keep up with world events, here's what happened: During the pairs finals, the Russian team of Elena Berezhnaya and Anton Sikharulidze made a number of flagrant errors, including these:

- Sikharulidze double-footed an axel landing. Or possibly he double-axeled a land footing. Whatever he did, it was flagrant.
- Sikharulidze also was wearing a disco shirt from 1978.

- During one of her spins, Berezhnaya can clearly be seen, in slow-motion video replay, taking a puff from a cigarette.

So everybody was sure the gold medal would go to the Canadian team of Jamie Sale and David Pelletier, who not only skated perfectly, but whose names are also much easier to spell. Yet the judges gave the gold to the Russians, a decision that had even the normally mellow Utahans screaming vicious profanities, Mormon-style ("What in the gosh darn HECK?!" "I'll be gum swizzled!" etc.).

How could this happen? To answer that question, we must understand how figure skating is judged. There are nine judges, broken down as follows:

- Judges from nations with plumbing: four
- Judges from former communist nations where the most reliable form of transportation is the yak: four
- French judges who hate everybody because the French never win anything: one

After each performance, the judges carefully weigh both the artistry and the technical merit. Then they vote for whomever they were going to vote for anyway. Usually they vote for skaters who are from their own country, or who have an established reputation. This is why in 1998 the Olympic gold medal for pairs figure skating went to a Russian team that had retired in 1996.

In the case of the 2002 pairs gold, all the plumbing-nation judges voted for the Canadians, and all the yak-nation judges voted for the Russians. The balance was tipped by the French judge, who later admitted she voted against the Canadians only because at the time she thought they were Americans, on the grounds that, quote, "they have good teeth."

So now we have an Olympic scandal, which has quickly burgeoned into an international crisis. Tensions soared on Thursday night when both the Canadian and Russian governments ordered their armed forces to go on highest alert; thankfully, things cooled down a few hours later when the two countries realized that they don't HAVE any armed forces.

But still, this scandal has cast a pall over figure skating, which must get its house in order if it is to be viewed as an untainted sport, like boxing. Fortunately, the International Skating Union has recognized the problem and is taking steps to correct it.

"We're going to have a thorough review of our judging procedures," stated the ISU. "This will be done by an outside firm with an impeccable reputation: Arthur Andersen."

Don't Trust Any Judge
with Two First Names

SALT LAKE CITY

Despite efforts to resolve the figure skating scandal, it continues to rage out of control here, at least in the media center, where riot police have been called in to quell fighting among roving gangs of Canadian, Russian, and French journalists. As of this morning, seventeen people had been treated for wounds inflicted by Bic pens.

The trouble stems from the now-infamous pairs competition, in which the gold medal was awarded to the Russians, despite the fact the clear winners were the pair from Canada, who have since become the most famous Canadians in world history, surpassing even (EDITOR: Please insert names of some famous Canadians here).

The judges' decision touched off a firestorm of outrage, with most of the attention focused on the French judge, Marie-

Reine Le Gougne. Among the highly suspicious facts that have come to light about her are:

1. She appears to have two first names.

2. The letters in "Marie-Reine Le Gougne" can be rearranged to spell "An eerie groin legume."

3. A person looking exactly like her can clearly be seen in the background of the Zapruder film.

The scandal became so huge that it threatened to tarnish the reputation of figure skating, which is not easy, since, ethically speaking, figure skating already has basically the same reputation as the Soprano family. And so on Friday, action was taken to restore the integrity of the sport. This action was taken by — get ready for some irony — the International Olympic Committee (motto: "No Longer Openly Accepting Bribes").

Specifically, the IOC ruled that:

1. The Russians will keep their gold medals for pairs figure skating.

2. A second set of gold medals for pairs figure skating will be awarded to the Canadians.

3. Henry L. Curdlicker, who drove the Zamboni machine, also will be given a gold medal for pairs figure skating.

4. The Trial Lawyers Association will file a class-action lawsuit on behalf of "the potentially millions of other people who might be entitled to receive gold medals in pairs figure skating."

5. The Oakland Raiders will be declared winners of the Raiders-Patriots playoff game, because a review of the videotape shows that, in the words of IOC president Jacques Rogge, "Brady clearly fumbled the ball."

6. The Eerie Groin Legumes would be a good name for a rock band.

Unfortunately, these actions have not ended the controversy. The Russians are furious because their gold medals are tainted. The Canadians are furious because *their* "gold medals," which the IOC had to purchase at the last minute from a local trophy store, are in fact plastic medallions labeled "FIRST PRIZE 1987 UTAH STATE FAIR BEST ZUCCHINI." The French are furious because they are French. The only happy group is the American press corps. As long as we can keep the scandal going, we get to stay indoors and write about it, instead of freezing our butts off watching the biathlon.

COMING TOMORROW: Kenneth Lay wins giant slalom.

Buses and Mucus: International Snits Become Inevitable

SALT LAKE CITY

The mood was cranky here in the waning moments of the 2002 Winter Games:

- RUSSIA threatened to walk out of the Olympics if it was not immediately awarded gold medals in women's figure skating, the Nordic combined alpine snowshoe and two events to be named later.
- KOREA threatened to walk out of the Olympics if it did not get whatever Russia got.
- LITHUANIA threatened to walk out of the Olympics if whoever stole its lucky towel did not return it.
- PORTUGAL actually did walk out of the Olympics, but nobody noticed, so Portugal sulked back into town and

spent the rest of the Games holed up in its hotel room watching dirty movies.

So basically the Winter Olympics degenerated into a great big international snit. This is what inevitably happens when you gather people from many different nations and force them to sit together for hours in crowded buses, listening to each other's ongoing efforts to expel mucus clots. I don't want to get too explicit, but the dry, cold atmospheric conditions here tend to result in nasal formations the size of Yorkshire terriers.

Some nations were so angry that they threatened not only to leave these Olympics, but also to boycott the 2004 Summer Games, scheduled to be held in Greece. As you can imagine, this caused great consternation in Greece, which issued the following statement: "The Olympics are coming HERE??"

But the immediate issue was not whether Greece will be ready to host the 2004 Games (no). The immediate issue was how to make the snitting nations happy, especially the Russians. The Olympic movement simply cannot allow the Russians to become estranged, because Russia is a vital part of the world sports community, in the sense of having nuclear missiles.

And the Russians were REALLY hacked off, for a bunch of reasons. First, they lost the Cold War. THEN they were forced to share the gold medal for pairs figure skating with Canada. THEN one of the top Russian cross-country skiers was disqualified because, in the words of Olympic drug-testing officials, "her urine sample burst into flames."

But the last straw came Thursday night, when Russia's top woman figure skater, the veteran Irina Slutskaya, lost the gold medal to an American, Sarah Hughes, who is maybe eleven years old and who passed the time, while waiting for her scores to appear, playing with her Olympics Barbie.

The Russians protested the women's result, but to no avail. The International Olympic Committee interviewed the judges, who pointed out, correctly, that the letters in "Irina Slutskaya" can be rearranged to spell "Russian Yak Tail." This is a mandatory two-tenths deduction.

The situation was finally resolved Friday when, after a lengthy meeting with IOC officials, the Russians agreed to drop their gold-medal demands and remain in the Games. In return for this act of sportsmanship, they will get East Germany back. So everything came out fine. Speaking of which, I need to blow my nose.

The next section of this book presents a selection of my regular weekly columns. I use this platform to address issues that I believe are of concern to the nation and the world, such as taxes, the economy, and what, exactly, the Lone Ranger shouted as he rode away.

In a Battle of Wits with Kitchen Appliances, I'm Toast

Recently the *Washington Post* printed an article explaining how the appliance manufacturers plan to drive consumers insane.

Of course they don't SAY they want to drive us insane. What they SAY they want to do is have us live in homes where "all appliances are on the Internet, sharing information" and appliances will be "smarter than most of their owners." For example, the article states, you would have a home where the dishwasher "can be turned on from the office" and the refrigerator "knows when it's out of milk" and the bathroom scale "transmits your weight to the gym."

I frankly wonder whether the appliance manufacturers, with all due respect, have been smoking crack. I mean, did they ever stop to ask themselves WHY a consumer, after loading a dishwasher, would go to the office to start it? Would there be some kind of career benefit?

YOUR BOSS: What are you doing?

YOU (tapping computer keyboard): I'm starting my dishwasher!

YOUR BOSS: That's the kind of productivity we need around here!

YOU: Now I'm flushing the upstairs toilet!

Listen, appliance manufacturers: We don't NEED a dishwasher that we can communicate with from afar. If you want to improve our dishwashers, give us one that senses when people leave dirty dishes on the kitchen counter, and shouts at them: "PUT THOSE DISHES IN THE DISHWASHER RIGHT NOW OR I'LL LEAK ALL OVER YOUR SHOES!"

Likewise, we don't need a refrigerator that knows when it's out of milk. We already have a foolproof system for determining if we're out of milk: We ask our wives. What we could use is a refrigerator that refuses to let us open its door when it senses that we are about to consume our fourth Jell-O Pudding Snack in two hours.

As for a scale that transmits our weight to the gym: Are they NUTS? We don't want our weight transmitted to our own EYEBALLS! What if the gym decided to transmit our weight to all these other appliances on the Internet? What if, God forbid, our refrigerator found out what our weight was? We'd never get the door open again!

But here is what really concerns me about these new "smart" appliances: Even if we like the features, we won't be able to use them. We can't use the appliance features we have NOW. I have a feature-packed telephone with 43 buttons, at least 20 of which I am afraid to touch. This phone probably can communicate with the dead, but I don't know how to operate it, just as I don't know how to operate my TV, which has features out the wazooty and requires THREE remote controls. One control (44 buttons) came with the TV; a second (39 buttons) came with the VCR; the third (37 buttons) was brought here by the cable-TV man, who apparently felt that I did not have enough buttons.

So when I want to watch TV, I'm confronted with a total of 120 buttons, identified by such helpful labels as PIP, MTS, DBS, F2, JUMP, and BLANK. There are three buttons labeled POWER, but there are times — especially if my son and his friends, who are not afraid of features, have changed the settings — when I honestly cannot figure out how to turn the TV on. I stand there, holding three remote controls, pressing buttons at random, until eventually I give up and go turn on the dishwasher. It has been, literally, years since I have successfully recorded a TV show. That is how "smart" my appliances have become.

And now the appliance manufacturers want to give us even MORE features. Do you know what this means? It means that some night you'll open the door of your "smart" refrigerator, looking for a beer, and you'll hear a pleasant, cheerful voice — recorded by the same woman who informs you that Your Call Is Important when you call a business that does not wish to speak with you personally — telling you: "Your celery is limp." You will not know how your refrigerator knows this, and, what is worse, you will not know who else your refrigerator is telling about it ("Hey Bob! I hear your celery is limp!"). And if you want to try to make the refrigerator STOP, you'll have to decipher Owner's Manual instructions written by and for nuclear physicists ("To disable the Produce Crispness Monitoring feature, enter the Command Mode, then select the Edit function, then select Change Vegetable Defaults, then assume that Train A leaves Chicago traveling westbound at 47 miles per hour, while Train B . . .").

Is this the kind of future you want, consumers? Do you want appliances that are smarter than you? Of course not. Your appliances should be DUMBER than you, just like your furniture, your pets, and your representatives in Congress. So I am urging you to let the appliance industry know, by phone, letter, fax, and e-mail, that when it comes to "smart" appliances, you vote NO. You need to act quickly. Because while you're reading this, your microwave oven is voting YES.

Camping at Wal-Mart Parking Lot Is Survival of Fittest

I was in my house, which sits safely on the ground and does not have wheels, when I got a call from my editor, John.

He said: "We want you to spend the night in a recreational vehicle in the Florida City Wal-Mart parking lot."

I said: "What?"

John explained that Wal-Marts all around the nation had become popular overnight spots for RVers. He wanted me to check this out. That's what editors do: They think up things for reporters to do, and then they go home to sleep in their nice, safe beds, oblivious to the danger that their reporters may be facing as they fight to stay alive in the Wal-Mart parking lot, armed with nothing but their skill and their courage and their bare hands and their corporate credit card and a vehicle the size of a ranch home.

111

Fortunately, I happen to be the type of rugged individual who is not afraid of risk. I don't mean to brag, but, in the past three years alone, I personally have read two nonfiction books about people climbing Mount Everest. I would consider climbing Mount Everest myself, if there were a way to do it in a recreational vehicle.

And so it was that on Friday afternoon I rented a twenty-nine-foot RV equipped with the bare essentials of survival: air conditioning, a toilet, a shower, a stove, a microwave and, of course, color television. I drove the RV to my house, where my wife and I loaded it with our baby daughter and a whole bunch of diapers. We did this quickly, because our house is located in Coral Gables, where the penalty for being caught with a recreational vehicle in your driveway is death.

When we were ready, I took a last look at my house, started the RV engine, put it into gear, and pressed down on the accelerator. Roughly forty-five seconds later, the RV began to move forward, six tons of raging inertia.

We motored south on U.S. 1 for a piece (one piece equals 24.7 miles), stopping only once to buy gasoline. We arrived at the Florida City Wal-Mart around dusk, with the last, reddish rays of the setting sun magically transforming the parking lot from a vast expanse of gray asphalt into a vast expanse of gray asphalt that was also slightly reddish. We parked in front of the store, where we had an excellent view of its distinctive sign, which says, simply, WAL-MART.

A few other RVers were camped nearby; other than that, there was nobody there except for us, and the night sky, and the traffic on U.S. 1, and the hundreds of people who constantly pull into and out of the Wal-Mart parking lot twenty-four hours a day. As night fell, we began to get hungry. We knew that unless we found food, and found it quickly, we could die of starvation within a matter of weeks. We felt that we had no choice but to go to the Wal-Mart store.

We crossed the parking lot on foot, following a route I had scouted earlier. Once inside the store, we realized that we might never find our way back out, because it is *enormous*, with a structure that covers 224,000 square feet. (In comparison, the state of Vermont covers only 217,000 square feet.) The Wal-Mart aisles go on forever, and if you wander far enough, you will find virtually everything a consumer could want — clothes, tents, tires, a bank, appliances, a beauty parlor, everything. On one aisle, there was a huge sign that said: SEE OUR SPORTING GOODS DEPARTMENT FOR ALL YOUR FROZEN BAIT NEEDS.

The Wal-Mart also boasts a vast food department, featuring enough cholesterol in the snack section alone to finish off every heart patient on Earth. It took us ten minutes just to decide on what kind of Vienna sausages we needed (spicy barbecue).

Finally, when we had what we hoped would be enough food (about seventy-five pounds) to get us through the night, we made our way back to the RV. We were just starting to feel confident about our chances of survival, when suddenly we made the kind of chilling discovery that turns an expedition into a nightmare: *The TV received only one channel.* Fortunately, it turned out to be the channel that was showing the NBA finals. I hate to think what we would have been reduced to otherwise. Cannibalism, probably.

After the game, we turned out the lights and fell asleep to the gentle, natural sound of shoppers putting merchandise into their car trunks. Our sleep was uninterrupted, except for the 527 times our daughter woke up demanding to be fed.

At dawn Saturday, I peeked out through the RV window blinds and watched the sun's first rays reflecting off the Wal-Mart store. A man was coming out, carrying a bag, perhaps containing his frozen-bait needs. I decided to go back to the store for coffee. It's dangerous to go into a Wal-Mart when you're not fully alert; you could easily come out with a pontoon boat.

But I escaped with just the coffee, and in a few minutes we had the RV packed up and lurching toward home.

We were tired, but proud. We'd survived a full night on one of the larger parking lots in South Florida.

That kind of experience really helps you find out what you're made of. In my case, Vienna sausage.

War on Smoking Always Has Room for Another Lawyer

Just when you think the War on Smoking cannot possibly get any more entertaining, up pops a new batch of lawyers to save the day.

Before I tell you about the latest legal wrinkle, let's review the key points in the War on Smoking so far:

POINT ONE: Cigarettes are evil, because smokers smoke them and consequently become sick or dead.

POINT TWO: The tobacco companies are evil, because they make and sell cigarettes.

POINT THREE: Therefore, in 1998 there was a big settlement under which the tobacco companies, by way of punishment for making and selling cigarettes, agreed to pay more than $200 billion to forty-six states and numerous concerned lawyers.

POINT FOUR: The tobacco companies

are paying for this settlement by making and selling cigarettes as fast as humanly possible.

POINT FIVE: At the time of the settlement, the states loudly declared that they would use the money for programs to eliminate smoking, which is evil.

POINT SIX: Perhaps you believe that the states are actually using the money for this purpose.

POINT SEVEN: You moron.

POINT EIGHT: In fact, so far the states are spending more than 90 percent of the tobacco-settlement money on programs unrelated to smoking, such as building highways.

POINT NINE: This is good, because we need quality highways to handle the sharp increase in the number of Mercedes automobiles purchased by lawyers enriched by the tobacco settlement.

So, to boil these points down to a single sentence: The War on Smoking currently is a program under which states build highways using money obtained through the sale of cigarettes. Is everybody clear on that?

Good! Now let's move on to the entertaining new wrinkle. It seems that a new batch of lawyers, who were not involved in the original tobacco litigation, has been pondering the 1998 settlement, and they have come to the conclusion that it has a very serious legal flaw, namely: They are not getting any of the money.

Ha ha! That was just a joke, and I will instruct the jury to disregard it. The new lawyers are in fact unhappy because they believe the tobacco settlement unfairly leaves out a group of victims who deserve a hefty share of the money. And those victims are: smokers. That's right: Smokers, without whom there would not even BE a tobacco settlement, are not getting a piece of the pie! So the new lawyer batch believes that billions of dollars of the tobacco settlement should go to smokers who receive Medicaid for illnesses that they have suffered as a result of smoking.

I realize this sounds complicated, so let's break down the way the cash would flow if these new lawsuits are successful:

1. SMOKERS would give money to THE TOBACCO COMPANIES in exchange for cigarettes.

2. THE TOBACCO COMPANIES would then give the money to THE STATES (and their lawyers).

3. THE STATES would then give the money to SMOKERS (and their lawyers).

4. THE SMOKERS would then pre-

sumably give the money to THE TOBACCO COMPANIES in exchange for more cigarettes.

Perhaps you're thinking: Isn't this inefficient? Why not eliminate the middle steps and simply require tobacco companies to give cigarettes to smokers for free?

The trouble with that idea is that it would defeat the two main purposes of the War on Smoking, which are (1) to provide the states with money; and (2) to provide lawyers with, well, money. And this would be an especially cruel time to take the War on Smoking money away from the American lawsuit industry, which already suffered a devastating setback recently when the Y2K computer glitch, tragically, failed to be disastrous.

So we should not be critical of the way our political and legal leaders are waging the War on Smoking. They have proved once again that this great nation, with its "can-do" attitude, can take any problem, no matter how sad and hopeless it seems, and figure out a way to turn it into increased Mercedes sales. Although I do not mean to cynically suggest that the only beneficiaries of the War on Smoking are luxury-car dealerships. Learjets are also selling well.

Fill Out the Census
and Win Your
Own Bureaucracy

Unless you are hiding in a drain pipe, by now you should have received your census questionnaire from the federal government.

The census is a federal tradition dating back to 1790, when President Washington ordered all citizens to form a line and count off by ones, thus establishing that the U.S. population at that time was "eleventeen." In modern times, the census is taken by the Census Bureau every ten years, as required by the Constitution. (For the other nine years, Census Bureau employees play pinochle while remaining on Red Alert, in case the Constitution suddenly changes.)

How important is the census to us today? Here's a quote from a letter my household received from Kenneth Prewitt, director of the Census Bureau:

"Huwag ninyong sasagutin ang Inggles

na form na inyong tatanggapin sa koreo."

I did not make this quote up. More than half of Mr. Prewitt's letter to my household is written in various foreign languages. As far as I can tell, in this particular quote Mr. Prewitt is saying: "Anybody who gets sausage and eggs on the census form will end up (something bad) in South Korea." This is not a threat that the federal government makes lightly.

Why is the census so important? For one thing, it enables the government to locate its citizens so it can administer programs to them. The census also determines our congressional representation, which is very important. For example, in the 1990 census, a homeowner named Ward A. Frondflinger Jr. of Lawrence, Kansas, left his census form out on the dining-room table, and unbeknownst to him, his children filled it out and mailed it in, with the information that his household had 984 million members. Today, the Frondflingers are personally represented by twelve congresspersons and five U.S. senators, and they have their own naval base.

Contrast their situation with that of North Dakota, which, because of poor participation with the 1990 census, wound up reporting that it had a total of only seven residents (the actual number is believed to be much closer to nine). As a result, today North Dakota has zero representatives in Congress and may no longer even be part of the United States. (Somebody should go up there and check.)

So the "bottom line" is that it is in your best interest, as a citizen, to fill out your census form. Here's some information to help you:

Q. What kinds of questions does the census form ask?

A. Most citizens will receive the short form, which asks you only for basic information that the government needs to administer programs to you, such as your name, age, sex, race, weight, and whether or not you wear thong underwear.

Q. What if I get the long form?

A. You had better know something about calculus.

Q. Is my census information confidential?

A. Absolutely. Nobody is allowed to see your personal census information except federal employees and their friends.

Q. What are my choices regarding my race?

A. You may choose from any of the following federally approved races: Black,

White, Beige, Blush, Bisque, Asian, Latino, Caucasian, Person of Color, African American, Native American Indian, Spaniard, Original Hawaiian, Asian Minor, Native Alaskan, Person of Density, Indian Indian from India, Caucasian-Asian Hawaiian, Hispano-African-Alaskan Native Indian, Ohioan, Native Hawaiian Tourist, Munchkin, Italian Samoan, Wisenheimer, and Presbyterian. Or, if you prefer, you may invent your own race, and the government will create a large bureaucracy to keep track of you.

Q. Why does the government need this information?

A. That is none of your business.

Q. I have an imaginary friend named Mr. Wookins. Should I include him on my census form?

A. Of course. The federal government spends billions of dollars on imaginary programs; these must be targeted to reach the people who really need them.

Q. Is there a place on the census form where I can tell the government how much I hate these stupid low-flow toilets?

A. The government has provided margins for this express purpose.

Q. What will happen to me if I fail to

complete the census form?

A. In the words of Census Director Prewitt, "Matatanggap ninyo ang Tagalog na census form sa loob ng dalawang linggo."

Q. Can he DO that?

A. Do not tempt him.

Choice Between Death and Taxes Gets Easier and Easier

It's time for my annual Tax Guide, which takes you step-by-step through the federal filing process, from obtaining the proper tax forms all the way to getting that desirable upper prison bunk.

I'll start with an important reminder: This year, April 15 falls on a Saturday, which means that, by law, your tax return is due on *March 15,* which was several weeks ago. (This must be true, because it is being printed in a newspaper.) If you missed the deadline, the Internal Revenue Service says not to worry. "This is a totally understandable error made by many tax-payers," states IRS Commissioner Charles O. Rossotti. "They will be audited with meat hooks."

Here's another important reminder: As a taxpayer, you are required to be fully in compliance with the United States Tax

Code, which is currently the size and weight of the Budweiser Clydesdales. The Tax Code was written by Congress, although of course no member of Congress has ever actually read it; Congress has more important things to do, such as adding new regulations to the Tax Code. In fact, *nobody* has ever read all the way through the Tax Code. The last attempt to do so was made in 1987 by a squad of courageous volunteer Certified Public Accountants, accompanied by Sherpa guides. The last survivor made it as far as Section 2038–1239–0293.423.49.112.6 (b)(m), "Guidelines Concerning the Fiduciary Depreciation of the Pituitary Exemption for Certain Elk Parts." According to the coroner, what was left of his brain "looked like rancid mayonnaise."

Just for fun, let's look at an actual sentence from the Tax Code that I am not making up, sent in by alert CPA Paul Mangum:

"Notwithstanding paragraph (b)(1) of this section, a partnership, S corporation, or personal service corporation is considered a member of a tiered structure if the partnership, S corporation, or personal service corporation, or related taxpayers have organized or reorganized their ownership structure or operations for the principal purpose of obtaining a significant unintended tax benefit from making or continuing a section 444 election."

As a trained English major, I have read this sentence several times, and I THINK it's saying that if you deliberately try to obtain a benefit that you do not intend to obtain, then you belong in a "tiered structure." I have no idea what a "tiered structure" is, but it doesn't sound good. I picture a pyramid-shaped iron cage deep in the bowels of the IRS building, populated by spiders the size of fox terriers.

Some people have suggested that our tax laws should be simplified so that the taxpayers could actually understand them. How could this be done? My friend John Dorschner proposes this system: Every year, on April 15, all members of Congress would be placed in individual prison cells with the necessary tax forms and a copy of the Tax Code. They would remain locked in the cells, without food or water, until they had completed their tax returns and successfully undergone a full IRS audit. Of course this system would probably result in a severe shortage of congresspersons. But there might also be some drawbacks.

For the time being, however, you must

follow the current laws in preparing your return. So gather together your tax forms, your financial records, your calculator, and your three to five quarts of gin and get started! To guide you, here are the answers to some common tax questions:

Q. What are "capital gains"? How can I tell if I have them?

A. This requires a urine test.

Q. Recently, without realizing what was happening, and through no fault of my own, I accidentally married a multimillionaire on nationwide television. What are the tax implications of this?

A. You must file IRS Form 1092–348–498597–EZ, "Declaration of Total Bases Reached on Nuptial Night." An IRS spokesperson stated that "this kind of thing happens all the time" and noted that "generally all that happens is you lose your house."

Q. Speaking of television, when a contestant on *Who Wants to Be a Millionaire* wins the top prize, how long is it before he is contacted by the IRS?

A. IRS guidelines call for the first dog to clamp onto his leg while he is still hugging Regis.

Q. I understand that I can now file

my taxes electronically. How does that work?

A. It's easy! You simply fill out some forms on your computer, then log on to the Internet. Within seconds, all of your personal financial information is in the hands of a seventeen-year-old hacker known as The Data-Booger.

The IRS urges you to contact your congressperson at home late at night, and stresses that "you can fully deduct the cost of the ladder."

Don't Forget to Consider Feng Shui — and Other Deck Tips

Today's Do-It-Yourself Project Is: How to Build a Deck.

There's nothing like adding a deck to transform an ordinary home into a home attached to a mass of inexpertly nailed wood. And just imagine the family fun you'll have this summer with a deck!

"Come on, kids!" you'll call to your children. "Let's go out on the deck and have some fun!"

"Shut UP," they'll gaily reply, because they are engrossed in a Sony PlayStation video game that they've been playing for eleven consecutive weeks.

"Okay then!" you'll say, stepping out onto your new deck. "You kids are just going to miss out on all the AAIIIEEE." This is the noise you make when you pick up a splinter the size of a harpoon.

Yes, a deck would certainly be a great

addition to your home. But if you're like most people, you're reluctant to tackle such an ambitious project, for fear that you lack the "know-how" or will sever an important limb.

Well, you can stop worrying. For one thing, they are making amazing progress in the field of prosthetics. For another thing, building a deck is NOT as hard as you think! I've watched TV personality Bob Vila do it many times, and he is a regular "do-it-yourselfer" just like you, except that he has knowledge, skill, an unlimited budget, and a large staff of experts. So let's get started!

Step one is to select a site for your deck. You should do this in accordance with the principles of feng shui, an ancient Chinese philosophy whose name means, literally, "new fad." Feng shui (pronounced "wang chung") teaches us that where we locate our household items affects our happiness by controlling the flow of "ch'i," which is a life force that is always around us, everywhere, all the time, like Regis Philbin.

You may be skeptical, but feng shui is actually based on solid astrological principles that have been scientifically verified by Shirley MacLaine and other leading Californians. These people pay feng shui consultants serious money to come to their houses and tell them things like what direction their beds should be pointing. If you think I'm making this up, check out any feng shui publication, such as *Feng Shui for Modern Living* ("The World's Biggest Selling Feng Shui Magazine"), which is filled with useful tips, such as this one from the April issue: "Keep your toilet seat down . . . to prevent ch'i being unnecessarily 'flushed' away." (You know how true this is if you've ever had to pay a plumber to fix a toilet clogged by a big glob of escaped ch'i.)

My point is that, unless you want all your ch'i flowing onto your neighbor's driveway, you need to locate your deck in exactly the right place. In my experience, the ideal location for a deck, considering all factors, is: indoors. Just lay some boards on your living-room floor and tell everybody it's a deck. This way, you can enjoy your deck without going outdoors and turning yourself into essentially a Dunkin' Donuts for mosquitoes.

If you insist on having a traditional outdoor deck, follow these steps:

1. Go outside and, wearing steel-tipped work boots, carefully pace off an area the size of a deck.

2. Mark the corners by driving stakes

into the ground, using a No. 6 Whacking Hammer. If you hear screaming, you have lawn vampires, and you should call your Realtor immediately.

3. Drive to a giant mega-warehouse home-fixin's superstore that runs TV commercials wherein cheerful, knowledgeable employees help you find exactly what you need. Take beef jerky, as you will be wandering the aisles for days, because those commercials are a big pile of ch'i. You will need to purchase the following deck parts: beams, joists, posts, bevels, headers, footers, thrusters, barristers, and 8,000 metric feet of galvanized mahogany.

4. Nail these items together in the shape of a deck, as shown on the Bob Vila show.

That's all there is to it! Time to invite "the gang" over to enjoy some outdoor fun on your deck!

Important

SAFETY TIP: Send smaller, more expendable members of the gang out onto the deck before you try it.

NIGHTTIME SAFETY TIP: Everybody should wear garlic.

NEXT WEEK'S HOMEOWNER TOPIC: Faster Gardening Through Dynamite.

Was It "Hi-ho" or "Hi-yo," or Did the Lone Ranger Have a Lisp?

Here in the newspaper business (Motto: "Eventually, We WILL Find Your Driveway") we have a strict rule: We don't print ANYTHING unless we know it's true.

Except for the horoscope, of course. No offense, but if you take the horoscope seriously, your frontal lobes are the size of Raisinets. Also, some of the comics are not 100 percent accurate. For example, in real life, Garfield walks on four legs. He's a CAT, for gosh sakes!

Also, to be honest, many of us who work at newspapers don't hold the opinions that our newspapers express in the editorials. Some of us don't even know where these opinions come from. They just mysteriously appear, like Batman.

But basically, we try to be accurate. When we're writing our stories, we don't guess about facts. If we have ANY question, we thoroughly check the fact out by taking a poll of the journalists sitting around us in the newsroom.

For example, if we need the name of the U.S. secretary of state, we yell, "Anybody know the name of the U.S. secretary of state?" Then we listen to the various opinions of our cubicle neighbors. Only when we have carefully weighed their views do we proceed with writing the story ("The U.S. secretary of state, a short little lady possibly named 'Marge,' said today that . . .").

Yes, we have high standards for accuracy. That's why — despite all these new-fangled inventions such as the Internet, TV, the telegraph, etc. — surveys show that newspapers remain the most trusted source of news for consumers in the coveted demographic of People Who Are Dead or Older.

And that is why today I am deeply concerned about a letter I received from a concerned reader named Lloyd Peyton, who believes that I made a mistake in a column I wrote last year about my living room being infested by frogs. In this column, I quoted the Lone Ranger as saying: "Hi-ho, Silver, away!" According to Mr. Peyton, this is incorrect. He contends that the Lone Ranger said, quote, "Hi-yo, Silver, away!" — in other words, a "yo" instead of a "ho." Mr. Peyton says that having the Lone Ranger say "Hi-ho" is like having Santa Claus go "Yo! Yo! Yo!" This really stunned me, because I grew up watching the Lone Ranger, and I always believed that he said "Hi-ho." I never questioned this. What I DID question was how come he thought that putting on a little black mask would protect his Secret Identity. I mean, if you put on one of those masks, I guarantee you everybody will still know who you are (you are a dork wearing a mask). I had the same problem with Superman, who put on a pair of ordinary eyeglasses, and suddenly all the other characters thought he was a completely different person. (I bet they were BIG horoscope fans.)

Anyway, to settle the issue of "Hi-ho" vs. "Hi-yo," I contacted William Safire, who is the world's highest-ranking English-language authority who is willing to take my calls. He did not hesitate for a second.

"Hi-yo," he said. Next I checked with various professional newspaper editors, most of whom were certain, without even consulting their cubicle neighbors, that the Lone Ranger shouted "Heigh-ho." In my dictionary, "Heigh-ho" is defined as "an exclamation of mild surprise, boredom, disappointment, fatigue, greeting, etc." I find it hard to believe that this is the mood that the Lone Ranger wanted to convey to his horse moments after rounding up a passel of varmints. I also checked with various authors whom I happen to be in a very bad rock band with, including Amy Tan and Ridley Pearson, who both said "Hi-ho." (Amy noted, "In the dubbed version in China, it was 'Ai-yo, Shrivah!' ")

Stephen King said: "Hi-yo. I used it in *It* (my novel *It*, that is) and I'm sure. My brother thought it was 'Hi-Lo Silver, away,' but that makes zero sense."

Other responses from friends and relatives included "High ho," "Hiyo," "Ohio," and various versions that I cannot print in the newspaper, because they suggest that the Lone Ranger and Silver had perhaps spent a little too much time alone together, if you catch my drift. Anyway, having weighed the evidence, I now believe that I was incorrect, and that the Lone Ranger probably said "Hi-yo, Silver" as he rode off into the sunset with his faithful Indian companion, who, according to my cubicle neighbors, was named Madeleine Albright.

But now I'm wondering: If I was wrong

about the Lone Ranger, am I also wrong about what I believe the little boy on *Rin Tin Tin* yelled to call Rin Tin Tin ("Yo, Rinny!")? And what about what I believe was the Secret Yell that the boys on *Lassie* used to signal each other ("Kee-ah-kee!" answered by "Ki-yi-yi-yi!")? Am I wrong about EVERYTHING? If so, all I can say is, I'm in the right business.

Who Was That Masked Social Security Recipient?

TODAY'S ISSUE IN THE NEWS IS: Social Security.

Is Social Security safe? Experts tell us that unless we implement meaningful reform soon, the entire system will go bankrupt by the year 2050, plunging the nation into chaos and despair. I, personally, plan to be dead. So we don't need to worry about it.

Instead, let's talk about the ongoing debate over what, exactly, the Lone Ranger shouted to his horse, Silver, when he rode off into the sunset. As you may recall if you have no life, in a recent column I stated that I had always believed the Lone Ranger shouted "Hi-ho, Silver! Away!" But then I got a letter from a reader who insisted that the Lone Ranger shouted "Hi-yo, Silver! Away!" So I checked with top language experts including William Safire and Stephen King, and they agreed that it was, in fact, "Hi-yo," not "Hi-ho."

So I wrote a column endorsing the "Hi-yo" version, and I believed that the matter was settled. Little did I realize that I was opening a can of worms. Because it turns out that this issue is not so simple. There are many unanswered questions, including: Why did the Lone Ranger shout to a horse that was standing right under him? And why would anybody put worms into a can? And then why would anybody OPEN the can? (The same question could be asked about Spam.)

But getting back to "Hi-ho" vs. "Hi-yo": In response to my column, I received many letters from people who claim to have inside information about the Lone Ranger. I cannot print all of their letters here, but if you were to combine them into one generic letter, it would sound like this:

"Dear Mr. Barry: I am 263 years old, and I never missed an episode of the Lone Ranger on the electric radio, on top of which my aunt's cousin's dentist's husband once rode a bus with a man who knew the barber of a close friend of one of the show's original sagebrush wranglers, and I can state with absolute certainty that you are (*choose one:*) (a) absolutely correct; or

(b) a moron, because the Lone Ranger DEFINITELY shouted (*choose one:*) (a) 'Hi-yo, Silver!'; (b) 'Hi-ho, Silver!'; (c) 'Hi-o, Silver!'; (d) 'Heil, Silver!'; (e) 'It's Howdy Doody Time, Silver!' "

To buttress their arguments, people sent in reams of information from various sources regarding the Lone Ranger and his faithful Indian companion, Tonto. I have been poring over this information, and have extracted the following salient facts (I am not making these facts up):

- The original Lone Ranger show was created at Detroit radio station WXYZ in 1933. This explains why Tonto called the Lone Ranger "Kemo Sabe," a phrase that is derived from the name of a boys' summer camp in Michigan owned by the director's uncle.

- So when the Lone Ranger frowned in that thoughtful, serious manner of his, he may have been thinking: "I don't care HOW faithful he is; if he calls me a boys' summer camp in Michigan one more time, I'm going to put a silver bullet in his leg."

- One of the actors who portrayed the Lone Ranger on the radio was named Brace Beemer.

- The letters in "Brace Beemer" can be

rearranged to spell "Embrace Beer."

- According to the story line created by the radio writers, the Lone Ranger was the great uncle of the Green Hornet, a masked superhero who battled the forces of evil, and whose secret identity was Britt Reed, newspaper publisher.
- If you know anything about newspaper publishers, it is hard to imagine them battling any force more evil than a sand trap.
- The Green Hornet's faithful companion was named "Kato," whose namesake, Kato Kaelin, held the position of house-sitter for O. J. Simpson.
- In 1974, O. J. Simpson was in the movie *The Towering Inferno*, with Robert Wagner.
- In 1998, Robert Wagner was in *Wild Things*, with Kevin Bacon.

When we put all these facts together, we see that the question of exactly what the Lone Ranger shouted to his horse is a great deal more complex than we thought it was early in this column, before we decided to brace ourselves with a couple of beemers, if you catch our drift. Clearly what we need is for the president to appoint a federal commission, headed by the late Earl Warren, to examine the evidence and issue a report. Also, somebody needs to straighten out this Social Security mess. I've done all I can.

He Didn't Just Buy a House — He Bought a Home Repair Industry

We're moving. I blame my daughter. She's only five months old, but she has somehow acquired, at a conservative estimate, 250 million toys. Every morning, there seem to be more of them. I suspect they're having some kind of battery-powered sex while we sleep.

These toys make a lot of noise. In my youth, toys were passive lumps of wood or metal that were silent unless you whacked your brother on the head with them. But today's toys contain computer chips, so they can move and talk; this stimulates the mind of your child. Notice I say "your child." MY child just wants to eat the toys. For example, she has an electronic Pooh bear who moves his head and says things like, "Would you like to play with me?" This stimulates my daughter to try to put Pooh's head into her mouth. Any day now,

Pooh will hold up his paws and scream, "NOOOO!" But that will not stop my daughter. She is the Great White Shark of babies.

But my point is this: We have a smallish house, and we work at home, and it's hard to concentrate when the floor is covered with toys that are constantly trying to strike up conversations. So I called our Realtor and said: "We need to move."

Now a truly compassionate Realtor, upon hearing these words, would have shot me in the head. Instead, our Realtor found us a larger house. We liked it immediately, although it needed a Little Work.

"It just needs some paint," I told my wife. I can look at a house and know exactly what it needs, because in fifth and sixth grades I took Wood Shop.

So we had a Paint Guy look at the house. He told us — and we knew he was an expert, because he had a clipboard — that before he could paint it, it needed some carpentry work.

So we had a Carpentry Guy look at the house. He also had a clipboard.

"You see this?" he asked me, poking at a board. From my perspective, it looked no different from all the other boards in the house. From my perspective, the entire

HOUSE is random boards. But the Carpentry Guy was looking at this board with the facial expression of a man stuck in an elevator with the national leadership of the Big Flatulent Persons Support Group.

"When we take this board off," he said, ominously, "there's no telling WHAT we're gonna find."

I wanted to say, "So let's not take it off!" But I didn't want him to think that I was not a manly masculine Wood Shop graduate.

The Carpentry Guy said that, before he could start dismantling the house, we needed to have somebody look at our windows. So we had the Windows Guy come out. He was visibly shaken. I thought he was going to drop his clipboard. Apparently our windows have some kind of deadly window leprosy. They must be replaced immediately with new windows, which, to judge from the price and delivery date, will be made from gem-quality diamonds on another planet.

Did I mention the Termite Guy? No? Well, he believes that termites might be eating our house. So we are going to "tent" the house, which involves surrounding it with a giant tent, filling it with a deadly gas, and then having the homeowners crawl inside and mercifully kill themselves before they can write any more checks.

No, that would be wrong. We have a job to finish. To make our new house habitable, we have to contact the Roof Guy, the Electricity Guy, the Plumbing Guy, the Gas Guy, the Alarm Guy, the Tree Guy, the Moving Guy, and all the other guys THEY will want us to contact. The clipboard industry is depending on us!

Meanwhile, we need to sell our old house. When people come to look at it, we scurry around hiding any possessions that would suggest to a prospective buyer that we are not Martha Stewart. For example, in our bathroom (this is true) we hide the big bottle of Plax mouthwash. We want prospective buyers to think, "It's a nice house! And the owners apparently have had no problems with dental plaque!"

My big fear is that, when prospective buyers poke their heads into our daughter's room, the toys will start talking to them.

"These people are really slobs!" Pooh will shout. "They're hiding their Plax under the bathroom counter! Also, their daughter wants to eat my head!"

All I can say is, Pooh had better keep his fuzzy little mouth shut. Because I took Wood Shop. And I have a hammer.

How to Drive a Man Wild with Desire? Even a Stiff Breeze Works

When I'm in the supermarket checkout line, I always look at *Cosmopolitan* magazine to see if the editors have made any progress in their ongoing effort to figure out men.

I'm sure you're familiar with *Cosmopolitan* ("Fun — Fearless — Female"). It's the one with the cover that always has a picture of a woman who looks as though she has a prestigious and rewarding executive career as a hooker. Roughly half the articles in *Cosmopolitan* are devoted to explaining how you, the *Cosmo* reader, can make yourself look like the cover model. All you have to do is follow the two-step Cosmo Beauty Regimen:

STEP ONE: Using a combination of fun and fearless beauty procedures such as the Eyebrow Yank, the Hot Wax Torture, the Hydrochloric Acid Skin Peel, the Hoover Vacuum Home Spleen Removal, the Cage of Thigh-Eating Wolverines, and the Industrial Drain Cleaner Enema, you remove all of the physical elements that make you unattractive, such as your fat, hair, skin, fingerprints, and internal organs. At this point, you are essentially a skeleton with eyeballs, or, to put it another way, Ally McBeal.

STEP TWO: You smear your entire self with a complex system of foundations, bases, creams, lotions, gels, powders, moisturizers, conditioners, mousses, sprays, mascaras, eyeliners, lip glosses, enzymes, lacquers, organic papaya-enhanced roofing tars, etc., until you are encased inside an impenetrable layer of beauty products thick enough that there is no way for anybody to tell, without giving you a CAT scan, what you actually look like. You could be a Shetland pony under there.

Once you have achieved this fun and female "look," it's time for you to get started on the other topic that is discussed endlessly in *Cosmopolitan*: figuring out what men want. It's a tough one! *Cosmopolitan* editors wrestle with it day and night, and they're constantly announcing new breakthroughs. Pick up any issue, and you'll see articles like:

• "23 Ways to Drive Him Wild in Bed!"

- "127 Ways to Make Him Want to Get Naked Right in the Foyer!"
- "387 Ways to Make Him Completely Lose Biological Control of Himself While He Is Still in the Driveway!"

Over the decades, *Cosmopolitan* has printed literally thousands of surefire techniques for driving men insane with passion. If these techniques actually worked, by now the entire male population of the United States would have been wiped out by lust, literally exploding into little mushroom clouds of vaporized bodily fluids.

But this has not happened, except in the case of President Clinton. The problem, I think, is that *Cosmopolitan* is making this issue way more complicated than it actually is. I mean, we're talking about MEN here. You don't need rocket science to drive them wild in bed: All you need to do is to get in there with them. Or, just leave them alone for a while. Because men don't need much. Using a complex, sophisticated technique to get a man excited is like preparing a gourmet French meal for a Labrador retriever.

So I think *Cosmopolitan* is trying too hard. In fact, it may be doing women more harm than good. For example, the August issue has a feature titled "What to Say to

Make Him Ache for You — Whisper these frisky phrases if you wish to drive him wild." One of the frisky phrases *Cosmopolitan* advises you to whisper to men is — really — "We'd better hurry home, because at midnight I turn into a vixen." This frisky phrase might actually alarm the man, especially if he knows that the dictionary defines "vixen" as "an ill-tempered, shrewish, or malicious woman." Basically, you're telling the man he could suddenly find himself in bed with Lorena Bobbitt.

Another frisky phrase suggested by *Cosmopolitan* is — get ready — "My bikini waxer went a little overboard." Listen, women: If you actually say those words to a man, he's going to assume you want him to take you to the Emergency Room.

So my advice to the editors of *Cosmopolitan* is: Just drop this subject for a while. Trust me: Even without technical advice from you, your women readers will have no trouble getting men excited, as long as the men are aware (and believe me, they are) that the women, underneath their clothes, are not wearing clothes.

And consider this: If you *Cosmopolitan* editors stopped obsessing about men, you could focus your brainpower on the Middle East Peace Process, health care,

Social Security, or the federal budget surplus. I bet you could give us some important insights into these issues! Or at least tell us how to drive them wild in bed.

Your Child Deserves
a Halloween Costume
by Calvin Klein

Halloween is coming, and you parents know what that means! It means it's time for you to make fun and creative costumes for your kids! Otherwise you are not as good as the other parents.

Even as you read these words, competing parents — the kind of people whose homes have candles burning in front of statues of Martha Stewart — are hunched over their workbenches, creating costumes that require more time and effort than you spent planning your wedding. These are the parents you see on the "home and family" segments of morning TV shows just before Halloween:

HOST: Our next parent is Mrs. Shirley Hamperwinkle, who has dressed her daughter, Tiffany, as an exact replica of the Eiffel Tower! What an amazing costume! However did you do it, Shirley?

PARENT: Well, Sue, first I forged 12,000 miniature steel girders in my home blast furnace, using ore I dug out of my garden. I assembled these girders using 2.5 million tiny handmade rivets with the help of my husband, Ed, before he ran off. Then I attached the tower to Tiffany using 147 surgical screws.

HOST: But how does she take the costume off?

PARENT (becoming agitated): Take it off? Take it OFF?? WHY WOULD SHE TAKE IT OFF???

This is the kind of parent you're up against. So you can't just throw some half-baked costume together at the last minute, the way we did in my childhood, when 80 to 90 percent of us kids stumbled around blindly on Halloween night wearing bed sheets with poorly aligned eye holes. We were supposed to look like ghosts, although this never made a ton of sense to me. I mean, ghosts are the spirits of dead people, right? Why would dead people wear bed sheets? Did they all die in an explosion at a hotel laundry?

I preferred to trick-or-treat as a vampire, which I felt was much scarier. The problem was the plastic vampire teeth. I have a powerful gag reflex, so when people opened their doors, instead of being terrified by the awesome bone-chilling specter of the Prince of Darkness, they'd see this short, caped person, retching. Their only terror was that I might throw up on their shoes.

But getting back to my point: As a modern parent, you need to get to work on your children's costumes RIGHT NOW. Don't worry if you're not the "artsy" type! Because I have a really original and creative costume idea for you. Start by gathering together the following arts-and-crafts materials:

1. Car keys.
2. Money.

Okay! Now drive to the mall and buy your child a creative and original costume that was originally created in a factory in Taiwan. You'll have lots of choices! For little boys, you may choose from the following: Superman, Batman, Spider-Man, the X-Men, Licensed Character Man, Buzz Lightyear, Darth Maul, Rex Kilometer, Commander Strafe, Buck Gouge, Sergeant Groin, the Violence Squadron, the Legion of Compound Fractures, the Masters of Really Hard Face Punching, and Al Gore. For little girls you may choose among the following: Ballerina

Barbie, Princess Barbie, Cheerleader Barbie, Presidential Intern Barbie, Bride Barbie, Severe Hangover Barbie, Minority Group Barbie, Joint Chiefs of Staff Barbie, Chest-Cavity-Dwelling Alien Fetus Barbie, the Barbie Formerly Known as Barbie, and Al Gore.

Now your kids are all set for some real "trick-or-treat" fun! But before you let them leave the house, the U.S. Department of Consumer Nervousness reminds you to follow these important:

HALLOWEEN SAFETY RULES
- Be aware that many municipalities have established special dates for trick-or-treating. For safety reasons, these dates are never on Halloween. Some of them are closer to Easter.
- Make sure each child is carrying a fire extinguisher and wearing a head-mounted smoke detector.
- Trick-or-treat candy may have been tampered with, so you should take it away from your children, check it carefully, then eat it.
- Never allow your children to trick-or-treat at night, or in dangerous areas such as outdoors.

Remember: The important thing is to

have fun in a safe and federal manner. Even you adults can join in the Halloween fun! Why not think of a clever and topical costume: For example, if you're a fat, hairy man, you can walk around naked; if the police stop you, simply explain that you're trick-or-treating as the guy who won the million dollars on *Survivor*. I'm sure the police will applaud your cleverness! Then they'll take you to a place where you can make your one phone call. To Defense Attorney Barbie.

100 Years of Solitude, Waiting for Customer Service

Recently I had a great idea while waiting on hold for Customer Service. That's pretty much all I do these days: wait for Customer Service. My call is important to them. They have told me this many times in a sincere recorded message. They can't wait to serve me! They will answer my call just as soon as they finish serving the entire population of mainland China.

It's my own darned fault that I need to speak to Customer Service. We made a really stupid homeowner mistake: We moved to another house. Don't ever make this mistake! It's ALWAYS better to stay in your current house, even if it's actively on fire. If other people have bought your house and are moving in, you should hide in the basement and forage for food at night.

Because if you move, you'll end up like us: surrounded by hundreds of cardboard boxes packed by strangers, each box containing an average of one item — perhaps a used toothpick — wadded up inside 75,000 square feet of packing paper. Virtually every box will be labeled with some mutant spelling of the word *miscellaneous*. You will not be able to find ANYTHING. For example, I'm pretty sure that, before we moved, we had a seven-month-old daughter.

(I'm kidding, of course. We know exactly where our daughter is. She's inside of one of these boxes.)

On moving day, I was crouching in a forest of stacked boxes, attempting to take apart a sleeper-sofa the size of a Chevrolet Suburban so that we could attempt to force it through a doorway the width of Courteney Cox, when suddenly, outside, I heard the movers, who spoke Spanish, shouting something about a *"serpiente."* I could tell by the urgency in their voices that there were upside-down exclamation points at the beginnings of their sentences. So I ran outside, and there, on the front walk, was a snake. In other places, when you move, you're visited by the Welcome Wagon; here in South Florida, you get: the Welcome Snake!

"I'm always around!" was the snake's unspoken message. "Let me know if you ever need any puncture wounds!"

But my point, which I am hoping to get to before we reach the end of the column, is that, because we moved, we had to change all the essential services — the electrical service, the phone service, the mail service, the water service, the cable service, the beer tanker delivery service, etc. — and naturally, because all the companies involved use sophisticated computers, none of these services actually works right in our new house. Everything is mixed up. We have water coming from our phone, and we receive phone calls on our toaster, and when we turn on our kitchen faucet, scenes from *Buffy the Vampire Slayer* come gushing out.

So to straighten this mess out, I quit doing my job (whatever that may be) and started spending my days waiting on hold for Customer Service, listening to the snappy "lite" jazz music they play when they are not telling you how important your call is to them. While doing this, I got my idea. You know those telemarketing people who always call you at dinnertime? I'm talking about the ones who never come right out and say they're selling something. Lately, they've been using the bizarre term "courtesy call" to describe what they're doing.

"Mr. Barry," they'll say, "this is just a courtesy call to do you the courtesy of interrupting your dinner so I can ask you this question: Would you like to save fifty percent or more on your long-distance phone bill?"

I always say no. I tell them that I WANT a big long-distance bill, and that I often place totally unnecessary calls to distant continents just to jack it up. I tell them that if my long-distance bill is not high enough to suit me, I deliberately set fire to a pile of cash. Then I hang up. But of course this does not stop them. The next night, they call again. That's how courteous they are.

So here's the deal: On the one hand, we have telemarketing people constantly calling us, despite the fact that everyone hates them, and to my personal knowledge nobody in the history of the world has ever bought anything from them; and on the other hand, when we want to reach Customer Service, we can never get through. Obviously, what corporate America needs to do is round up all the employees in the Telemarketing Department, march them over to Customer Service, and order them to step over the bodies of the Customer

Service employees, all of whom apparently passed away years ago, and ANSWER THE PHONE, okay? Because this toaster is burning my ear.

Don't Fear to Tread:
Laying Tile Just Requires
Stick-to-itiveness

TODAY'S TOPIC FOR HOMEOWNERS IS: How to install a tile floor.

Any home decorator will tell you that there is nothing quite like a tile floor for transforming an ordinary room into an ordinary room that has tile on the floor.

But if you're like most homeowners, you think that laying tile is a job for the "pros." Boy, are you ever stupid! Because the truth is that anybody can do it! All it takes is a little planning, the right materials, and a Fire Rescue unit.

Consider the true story of a woman in Linthicum, Maryland, who decided to tile her kitchen floor, as reported in an excellent front-page newspaper article written by Eric Collins for the Sept. 26 issue of the Annapolis, Maryland, *Capital*, and sent in by many alert readers. According to this article, the woman, who wanted to be identified only as "Anne" for reasons that will become clear, decided to surprise her fiancé by tiling her kitchen floor herself, thus saving the $700 a so-called "expert" would have charged for the job.

Step 1, of course, was for Anne to spread powerful glue on the floor, so the tiles would be bonded firmly in place. Anne then proceeded to Step 2, which — as you have probably already guessed — was to slip and fall face-first into the glue coat she created in Step 1, thus bonding herself to the floor like a gum wad on a hot sidewalk.

Fortunately, Anne was not alone. Also in the house, thank goodness, was one of the most useful companions a person can ever hope to have: a small dog. Specifically, it was a Yorkshire Terrier, a breed originally developed in England to serve as makeup applicators. A full-grown "Yorkie" is about the size of a standard walnut, although it has more hair and a smaller brain.

Anne's dog — named Cleopatra — saw that her owner was in trouble, so she immediately ran outside and summoned a police officer.

Ha ha! No, seriously, Cleopatra did what all dogs do when their owners are in trouble: lick the owner's face. Dogs believe this is the correct response to every emergency. If Lassie had been a real dog, when little Timmy was sinking in the quicksand, Lassie, instead of racing back to the farmhouse to get help, would have helpfully licked Timmy on the face until he disappeared, at which point Lassie, having done all she could for him, would have resumed licking herself.

So anyway, when Cleopatra decided to help out, she naturally also became stuck in the glue. But again, luck was on Anne's side, because also at home were her two daughters, ages nine and ten, who, realizing that the situation was no joking matter, immediately, in the words of the *Capital* article, "began laughing hysterically."

Eventually, with their help, Anne got unstuck from the floor and was able to lay the tile. But she still had glue all over herself. So, according to the *Capital* article, "she called a glue emergency hotline, but no one answered."

I don't know about you, but that sentence disturbs me. I think somebody should check on the glue emergency hotline staff.

I picture an officer reeking of glue fumes, with whacked-out workers permanently bonded to floors, walls, ceilings, each other, etc. Come to think of it, this is also how I picture Congress.

But getting back to Anne: Still trying to solve her personal glue problem, she called a tile contractor. During this conversation, the glue on her body hardened, such that (1) her right foot became stuck to the floor, (2) her legs became stuck together, (3) her body became stuck to a chair, and (4) her hand became stuck to the phone.

"I had to dial 911 with my nose," she is quoted as saying.

When the rescue personnel arrived, they found Anne still stuck.

Perhaps this is a good time in our story to bring up the fact that she had been working in, and was still wearing, only her underwear.

Fortunately, the rescue crews were serious, competent, highly trained professionals, and thus, to again quote the *Capital* article, they "laughed until they cried."

Once they recovered, the rescue crews were able to free Anne by following the standard procedure for this type of situation: licking her face.

No, seriously, they freed her with solvents, and everything was fine. Anne got her new floor and saved herself $700, which I am sure more than makes up for suffering enough humiliation to last four or five lifetimes.

So the bottom line, homeowners, is this: Don't be afraid to tackle that tile job! Just be sure to have a dog handy, and always remember the No. 1 rule of tile-installation professionals: Wear clean underwear.

Terror on Flight 611 — There's a Baby on Board, Ready to Shriek

Recently, my wife and I took our eight-month-old daughter on a trip involving five plane flights in one week. Many people would be reluctant to travel with a baby that small, but we had a compelling reason: We have Fig Newtons for brains.

An intelligent person, or even a reasonably bright fungus, would know that two people cannot possibly carry both a baby and all the supplies the baby needs, including stroller, car seat, clothes, diapers, industrial-sized bale of wipes, stuffed bear, stuffed tiger, stuffed frog, stuffed paramecium, etc. The total weight of all these supplies can be hundreds of times the weight of the actual baby. This is why your famous explorers rarely traveled with babies. If Magellan had tried to sail around the world with a baby on board, his ship would have sunk at the dock from the weight of the formula alone.

We were one of those wretched traveling families you see getting on planes — the kind where you don't actually see the people, just this mound of baby equipment shuffling slowly down the aisle toward you. This sight is always hugely popular with the other passengers, some of whom will yank open the emergency exits and dive out of the plane. Because they know what babies do on planes: They stand on their parents' laps and stick their heads up over the seats, so they can get maximum range when they shriek. On a baby-intensive airplane, you see shrieking baby heads constantly popping up all over, like prairie dogs from hell.

As a parent in this situation, your fervent hope is that the other babies on the plane will shriek louder than yours, thereby diverting passenger hatred away from you. It would not surprise me to learn that some parents creep under the seats and pinch other people's babies to set them off. I myself would never do such a thing. I carry a slingshot.

The trick for keeping your baby from crying on the plane is to come up with a new activity each time the baby gets bored. A standard baby gets bored every fifteen seconds, so on a four-hour flight, you, as a parent, need to come up with 960 different activities. By the third hour of the flight, your standards are pretty low. Baby wants to play in the airplane toilet? Sure! Baby wants to crawl into the cockpit and bite the navigator on the ankle? Whatever baby wants!

Here's what a stupid parent I am: On our first flight, I brought two newspapers on board. I did not read one word of either one. What I read was a book called *Farm Faces*, which is made entirely of cloth. There's a cow on the cover, and each page has a new animal. Here's the entire text: "chick," "lamb," "pig," "duck," "horse," "worm." I read this book to my daughter maybe forty times, using a dramatic and excited voice to show her how fascinating it was. I mean, talk about a surprise plot twist! I NEVER would have guessed worm!

I also tried to interest Sophie in the inflight movie, which was *The Perfect Storm*, in which George Clooney goes to sea in a fishing boat and is killed by special effects. Sophie did not care for it. I could see her point: I thought *Farm Faces* was less formulaic.

It goes without saying that your baby

will poop massively on the plane. This must have something to do with atmospheric pressure, because it never fails. Each year, more baby poop is produced on airplanes than in all of Portugal. Fortunately, most planes have a little changing shelf in the bathroom, which is the perfect size for a baby, provided that it is a baby gerbil. For human babies, you have to use the seat, which then must be burned when the plane lands. The only really practical place to change a baby on an airplane would be on the wing but, of course, you can't take the baby out there. The other passengers would never let you back inside.

You know what we need? We need an airline just for people with babies (it could be called "Shrieking Prairie Dogs from Hell Airlines"). The planes would not have seats: Everyone would squat on the floor. The preflight safety lecture would consist of a demonstration of how to get a Lego out of a child's mouth. The in-flight meal would be Cheerios eaten off the floor. If the noise reached a certain decibel level, plastic tubes would automatically pop out of the ceiling to dispense liquid horse tranquilizer to the parents. The in-flight movie would be *Farm Faces*, starring George Clooney as Worm.

Humvee Satisfies
a Man's Lust
for Winches

It is time for our popular feature "Stuff That Guys Need." Today's topic is: the Humvee.

Most Americans became aware of the Humvee (military shorthand for HUgely Masculine VEEhickle) during the Gulf War, when U.S. troops, driving Humvees equipped with missile launchers, kicked Iraq's butt and taught Saddam Hussein a lesson that he would not forget for several weeks.

After the war, a few wealthy Californians got hold of Humvees. This led to some mishaps, most notably when Arnold Schwarzenegger, attempting to open his garage door, accidentally launched a missile. Fortunately, it landed in a noncelebrity neighborhood.

But once the "bugs" were ironed out, the Humvee became available for civilian purchase. I test-drove one recently thanks to my co-worker Terry Jackson, who is the *Miami Herald*'s automotive writer and TV critic. That's correct: This man gets paid to drive new cars AND watch television. If he ever dies and goes to heaven, it's going to be a big letdown.

When I arrived at Terry's house, there was a bright-yellow Humvee sitting in his driveway, covered with puddles of drool deposited by passing guys. In terms of styling, the Humvee is as masculine as a vehicle can get without actually growing hair in its wheel wells. It's a big, boxy thing with giant tires and many studly mechanical protuberances. It looks like something you'd buy as part of a toy action-figure set called "Sergeant Bart Groin and His Pain Platoon."

Terry told me this particular Humvee model cost $101,000, which sounds like a lot of money until you consider its features. For example, it has dashboard switches that enable you to inflate or deflate your tires *as you drive*. Is that cool, or WHAT? In a perfect guy universe, this feature would seriously impress women.

GUY: Look! I can inflate the tires as I drive!

WOMAN: Pull over right now, so we can

engage in wanton carnality!

Unfortunately, the real world doesn't work this way. I know this because when I took my wife for a ride in the Humvee, we had this conversation:

ME: Look! I can inflate the tires as I drive!

MY WIFE: *Why?*

Another feature that my wife did not appreciate was the winch. This Humvee had a SERIOUS winch in front ("It can pull down a house," noted Terry). There's nothing like the feeling of sitting in traffic, knowing that you have a MUCH bigger winch than any of the guys around you. Plus, a winch can be mighty handy in an emergency. Like, suppose some jerk runs you off the road into a ditch. After a tow truck pulls you out, you could find out where the jerk lives, then use your winch to pull down his house.

The Humvee also boasts an engine. Terry offered to show it to me, but I have a strict policy of not looking at engines, because whenever I do, a mechanic appears and says "There's your problem right there" and charges me $758. I can tell you this, however: The Humvee engine is LOUD. I picture dozens of sweating men under the hood, furiously shoveling coal as Leonardo DiCaprio and Kate Winslet run gaily past.

As for comfort: Despite the Humvee's ruggedness, when it's cruising on the highway, the "ride" is surprisingly similar to that of a full-size luxury sedan being dragged across a boulder field on its roof. But a truly masculine, big-winched man does not need comfort. All he needs is the knowledge that he can take his vehicle into harsh and unforgiving terrain. And I gave the Humvee the toughest challenge you can give a car in America. That's right: I drove it to a shopping mall just before Christmas.

Perhaps you think I was foolhardy. Well, people said that the Portuguese explorer Vasco da Gama was foolhardy, too, and do you remember what he did? Neither do I. But if he had not done it, I doubt that Portugal would be what it is today: a leading producer of cork.

And thus I found myself piloting the Humvee through the mall parking structure at roughly the speed of soybean growth, knowing that I was competing for the one available parking space with roughly 20,000 other motorists, but also knowing that ALL of them would have to stop their vehicles if they wanted to inflate or deflate their tires. The pathetic wimps! I could not help but cackle in a manly way. My wife was rolling her eyes at me, but by God I got us safely into and out of there, and I doubt that I used more than 300 gallons of fuel. So Saddam, if you're reading this, please send more.

Dead or Alive, Turkeys Can Fowl Up Your Life

It's almost Thanksgiving, a time for us to pause in our busy lives and remember, as the Pilgrims did so long ago, that an improperly cooked turkey can kill us.

Even a live turkey can be dangerous. I base this statement on an article that I am not making up from the March 14 *Pittsburgh Tribune-Review*, sent in by alert reader Dan Broucek, which begins as follows:

"A tom turkey crashed through the windshield of a dump truck early Monday in Butler County and struck a fighting posture with the surprised driver."

I didn't know that turkeys had a fighting posture. What do they do? Put up their dukes? But if they put up BOTH dukes, they'd topple over, right? Maybe they put up just one duke, and hop around on the other duke in a threatening fashion. Whatever they do, I'm sure it would be terrifying to see one of them doing it next to you in a dump truck.

Fortunately, the driver was able to escape and call the police, who responded swiftly, as they do whenever they hear the dreaded radio code 10–84 ("Turkey in Fighting Posture"). The turkey, which weighed twenty-five pounds, was apprehended by a state game official who, incredibly, let it go without pressing charges.

Now here is where our story gets alarming: According to articles (also sent in by Dan Broucek) from the March 16 and 17 *Pittsburgh Post-Gazette*, just two days after the dump-truck incident, a woman was getting out of her car-pool van in downtown Pittsburgh when something came plummeting out of the sky, missing her by inches, and splatted on the sidewalk. Can you guess what that something was? That's correct: a Pilgrim.

No, seriously, it was a turkey. Specifically, it was a twenty-five-pound tom turkey, which had apparently crashed into a skyscraper twenty floors above. We do not have to be Sherlock Holmes to figure out what happened. I mean, how many twenty-five-pound turkeys could there be in the Pittsburgh area answering to the name "tom"? Clearly this was the same turkey that went after the dump truck, and when all it received was a slap on the wrist (I am assuming here that turkeys have wrists), it developed a fatal blood lust, as wild animals so often do, for things with windows, and it decided to attack a sky-scraper. Remember that there was a time in this nation, centuries ago, when giant herds of these vicious predatory birds roamed the forests, duking it out with whatever dared to get in their way, and shaking their mighty wattles in triumph, knowing that they were the Masters of the Forest, and that "The Mighty Shaking Wattles" would be a good name for a rock band (specifically, the Rolling Stones).

This is why the American Poultry Manufacturers of America stress that, in selecting a Thanksgiving turkey, the No. 1 rule is, quote, "it should be a dead turkey." Look for one that has been frozen solid enough to deflect a .38-caliber bullet; if it doesn't, put it right back into the freezer and fire into the supermarket ceiling until the Poultry Manager brings you something more acceptable.

PREPARING THE TURKEY: Proper turkey preparation is critical because, according to the U.S. Department of Agriculture, more Americans die every year from eating improperly cooked turkey than were killed in the entire Peloponnesian War. This is because turkey can contain salmonella, which are tiny bacteria that, if they get in your bloodstream, develop into full-grown salmon, which could come leaping out of your mouth during an important business presentation.

This does NOT mean you can't serve turkey this Thanksgiving! It just means that you, personally, should not eat it.

Step one in preparing the turkey is to let it thaw (allow six to eight years). Step two is to reach your hand inside the slimy, dark chest cavity of the turkey and remove the giblets. Be careful, because you are intruding upon the territory of the deadly North American giblet snake, which can grow, coiled inside an innocent-looking 12-pound turkey, to a length of 55 feet. In one of the most horrifying moments in cooking history, one of these monsters attacked Julia Child during her live 1978 Thanksgiving TV special; it would have strangled her if she had not known exactly where to insert her baster. Few people who have seen this chilling footage have failed to order the videotape from PBS.

Assuming you get the giblets out safely, Step three is to cook the turkey until it reaches a minimum internal temperature of 7,500 degrees centigrade (check by feeling the turkey's wrist). You're all done! It's time to enjoy a hearty Thanksgiving dinner, just like the one enjoyed by the Pilgrims. None of whom are alive today.

By *the Way,* Those Turkey Snakes Have Giant Fangs, Too

In the newspaper business (motto: "Trust Us! We're English Majors!") we have high standards of accuracy. Before we print anything, we make sure that:

- We personally believe it's true, or
- A reliable source (defined as "a source wearing business attire") told us it's true, or
- Another newspaper, with a respectable newspaper name such as "The Fort Smidling Chronic Truncator" says it's true, or
- It's getting late and we need to print SOMETHING so we can go to the bar.

Despite these safeguards, newspapers are not perfect, as evidenced by the recent front-page *New York Times* story incorrectly identifying Gen. Colin Powell as "the capital of Guam." (He is, in fact, the capital of Vermont.) But what makes newspapers special is that, in the words of the great seventeenth-century editor Walter Cronkite, "When we mess up, we 'fess up."

That's why I want to correct an error I made recently in a column on preparing a Thanksgiving turkey. Specifically, I wrote that you should be careful when reaching inside the turkey, because:

". . . you are intruding upon the territory of the deadly North American giblet snake, which can grow, coiled inside an innocent-looking 12-pound turkey, to a length of 55 feet. In one of the most horrifying moments in cooking history, one of these monsters attacked Julia Child during her live 1978 Thanksgiving TV special; it would have strangled her if she had not known exactly where to insert her baster."

After that column appeared, I received a letter, which I am not making up, from a woman in Lima, Ohio, who stated:

"I have a friend that will not eat turkey now and is afraid to put her hand in the cavity to clean one. I tried to tell her it was humor and no way could a 12-lb. turkey hold a 55-foot snake, nor could Julia Child kill one with a baster. She is not to be consoled. Please write about this in the near future, so my friend can enjoy turkey again."

I also received a letter from a woman in Canada who said that her 83-year-old mother now refuses to eat turkey because "people were finding snakes in the internal cavity."

So it seems that my column inadvertently started an "urban myth," like the one about albino alligators in the New York sewers, or the one about the president of the United States being chosen by some "Electoral College."

To clear this up, I did some research on the Internet. I wish I'd done so sooner, because with just a few mouse clicks I was able to locate many photographs of naked people. After researching these for several days, I went to an Internet research site and typed in the words *turkey snakes;* this led me to a site called "Reptiles and Amphibians of Europe," where I learned that there is a snake, found in Turkey, called the Large Whip Snake, or, in Latin, "Coluber jugularis jugularis" (literally, "chronic truncator") that grows to a length of 120 inches. According to the description, this snake ". . . strikes with an open mouth . . . the recurved teeth are apparently very difficult to remove if lodged in the skin."

So I want to set the record straight about

184

reaching into turkey cavities: There is NO DANGER that a 55-foot snake will strangle you. The snake will be at most 10 feet long, and it will merely lodge its teeth permanently in your skin. My mistake!

This does not mean, however, that we should let our guard down regarding poultry. I say this in light of news reports, sent in by many alert readers, concerning a woman in Newport News, Virginia, who purchased a box of chicken wings at a fast-food restaurant that, in the interest of avoiding a lawsuit, I will call by the totally made-up name "FcFonald's." Inside the box, the woman found — you guessed it — Walter Cronkite.

No, seriously, she allegedly found a deep-fried chicken head. She alerted the media, which published photographs of the chicken head: It looks like Sen. Strom Thurmond, only with a more natural hairstyle. When I saw this, I got right back on the Internet, because I wanted to answer a question that has no doubt already occurred to you: Is there a band called the Chicken Heads? It turns out there is. Some band members dress as chickens, but before you dismiss them as a bunch of "wackos," bear in mind that other members dress as a giant carrot and a wedge of cheese. They have a song called *The Man Without Nostrils.*

I hope this clears up any confusion. If you have further questions, please write to me, c/o This Newspaper, 123 Main Street, Colin Powell, Vermont, 12345. I'll be at the bar.

A GPS *Helps a Guy* Always Know Where His Couch Is

I'm a big fan of technology. Most guys are. This is why all important inventions were invented by guys.

For example, millions of years ago, there was no such thing as the wheel. One day, some primitive guys were watching their wives drag a dead mastodon to the food-preparation area. It was exhausting work; the guys were getting tired just WATCHING. Then they noticed some large, smooth, rounded boulders, and they had an idea: They could sit on the boulders and watch! This was the first in a series of breakthroughs that ultimately led to television.

So we see that there are vital reasons why guys are interested in technology, and why women should not give them a hard time about always wanting to have the "latest gadget." And when I say "women,"

I mean "my wife."

For example, as a guy, I feel I need a new computer every time a new model comes out, which is every fifteen minutes. This baffles my wife, who has had the same computer since the Civil War and refuses to get a new one because — get THIS for an excuse — the one she has works fine. I try to explain that, when you get a new computer, you get exciting new features. My new computer has a truly fascinating feature: Whenever I try to turn it off, the following message, which I am not making up, appears on the screen:

"An exception 0E has occurred at 0028:F000F841 in VxD —. This was called from 0028:C001D324 in VxD NDIS(01) + 00005AA0. It may be possible to continue normally."

Clearly, this message is not of human origin. Clearly, my new computer is receiving this message from space aliens. I don't understand all of it, but apparently there has been some kind of intergalactic problem that the aliens want to warn us about. What concerns me is the last sentence, because if the aliens are telling us that "it may be possible to continue normally," they are clearly implying that it may NOT be possible to continue normally. In other words, the Earth may be doomed, and the aliens have chosen ME to receive this message. If I can figure out exactly what they're saying, I might be able to save humanity!

Unfortunately, I don't have time, because I'm busy using my new GPS device. This is an extremely important gadget that every guy in the world needs. It receives signals from orbiting satellites, and somehow — I suspect the "cosine" is involved — it figures out exactly where on the Earth you are. Let's say you're in the town of Arcola, Illinois, but for some reason you do not realize this. You turn on your GPS, and, after pondering for a few minutes, it informs you that you are in . . . Arcola, Illinois! My wife argues that it's easier to just ASK somebody, but of course you cannot do that, if you truly are a guy.

I became aware of how useful a GPS can be when I was on a plane trip with a literary rock band I belong to called the Rock Bottom Remainders, which has been hailed by critics as having one of the world's highest ratios of noise to talent. On this trip were two band members whom I will identify only as "Roger" and "Steve," so that you will not know that they are actually Roger McGuinn, legendary co-founder of the Byrds, and Stephen King, legendary legend.

We were flying from Chicago to Boston, and while everybody else was reading or sleeping, "Roger" and "Steve," who are both fully grown men, were staring at their GPS devices and periodically informing each other how far we were from the Boston airport. "Roger" would say, "I'm showing 238 miles," and "Steve" would say, "I'm showing 241 miles." Then "Roger" would say, "Now I'm showing 236 miles," and "Steve" would come back with another figure, and so on. My wife, who was confident that the airplane pilot did not need help locating Boston, thought this was the silliest thing she had ever seen. Whereas I thought: I NEED one of those.

So I got a GPS for Christmas, and I spent the entire day sitting on a couch, putting it to good use. Like, I figured out exactly where our house is. My wife told me this was exciting news. I think she was being sarcastic, but I couldn't be sure, because I had to keep watching the GPS screen, in case our house moved. I also used my GPS to figure out exactly how far my couch is from LaGuardia Airport (1,103 miles). There is NO END to the usefulness of this device! If you're a guy, you need to get one NOW, so you can locate yourself on the planet. While we still have one.

Road to Romantic Ruin
Paved with Chain Saws

The other day my son and I were talking, and the subject of women came up, and I realized that it was time he and I had a Serious Talk. It's a talk every father should have with his son; and yet, far too often, we fathers avoid the subject, because it's so awkward.

The subject I am referring to is: buying gifts for women.

This is an area where many men do not have a clue. Exhibit A was my father, who was a very thoughtful man, but who once gave my mother, on their anniversary, the following token of his love, his commitment, and — yes — his passion for her: an electric blanket. He honestly could not understand why, when she opened the box, she gave him that look (you veteran men know the look I mean). After all, this was the deluxe model electric blanket! With an *automatic thermostat!* What more could any woman WANT?

Another example: I once worked with a guy named George who, for Christmas, gave his wife, for her big gift — and I am not making this gift up — a chain saw. (As he later explained: "Hey, we NEEDED a chain saw.") Fortunately, the saw was not operational when his wife unwrapped it.

The mistake that George and my dad made, and that many guys make, was thinking that when you choose a gift for a woman, it should do something useful. Wrong! The first rule of buying gifts for women is: THE GIFT SHOULD NOT DO ANYTHING, OR, IF IT DOES, IT SHOULD DO IT BADLY.

For example, let's consider two possible gifts, both of which, theoretically, perform the same function:

GIFT ONE: A state-of-the-art gasoline-powered lantern, with electronic ignition and dual mantles capable of generating 1,200 lumens of light for ten hours *on a single tank of fuel.*

GIFT TWO: A scented beeswax candle, containing visible particles of bee poop and providing roughly the same illumination as a lukewarm corn dog.

Now to a guy, Gift One is clearly superior, because you could use it to see in the dark. Whereas to a woman, Gift Two is

MUCH better, because women love to sit around in the gloom with reeking, sputtering candles, and don't ask ME why. I also don't know why a woman would be ticked off if you gave her a 56-piece socket-wrench set with a 72-tooth reversible ratchet, but thrilled if you give her a tiny, very expensive vial of liquid with a name like "L'Essence de Nooquie Eau de Parfum de Cologne de Toilette de Bidet," which, to the naked male nostril, does not smell any better than a stick of Juicy Fruit. All I'm saying is that this is the kind of thing women want. (That's why the ultimate gift is jewelry; it's totally useless.)

The second rule of buying gifts for women is: YOU ARE NEVER FINISHED. This is the scary part, the part that my son and his friends are just discovering. If you have a girlfriend, she will give you, at MINIMUM, a birthday gift, an anniversary gift, a Christmas/Hanukkah/Kwanzaa gift and a Valentine's Day gift, and every one of these gifts will be nicely wrapped AND accompanied by a thoughtful card. When she gives you this gift, YOU HAVE TO GIVE HER ONE BACK. You can't just open your wallet and say, "Here's, let's see . . . seventeen dollars!"

And, as I told my son, it only gets worse.

Looming ahead are bridal showers, weddings, baby showers, Mother's Day, and other Mandatory Gift Occasions that would not even EXIST if men, as is alleged, really ran the world. Women observe ALL of these occasions, and MORE. My wife will buy gifts for NO REASON. She'll go into one of those gift stores at the mall that men never enter, and she'll find something, maybe a tiny cute box that could not hold anything larger than a molecule, and is therefore useless, and she'll buy it, PLUS a thoughtful card, and SHE DOESN'T EVEN KNOW WHO THE RECIPIENT IS YET. Millions of other women are out doing the same thing, getting farther and farther ahead, while we guys are home watching instant replays. We have no chance of winning this war.

That's what I told my son. It wasn't pleasant, but it was time he knew the truth. Some day, when he is older and stronger, we'll tackle an even more difficult issue, namely, what to do when a woman asks: "Do these pants make me look fat?" (Answer: Flee the country.)

Nice Words About the IRS on the Way to Leavenworth

Every year at tax time, I write a lighthearted "fun" column about the Internal Revenue Service, in which I make a lot of jokes that are not serious, because I am just kidding around in a humorous vein. The truth is that I have the deepest respect for the IRS, and for the thousands of fine men and women and Doberman pinschers who work there.

Ha ha! That's an example of the kind of good-natured "jab" I usually take at the IRS, stemming from affection, rather than hostility. Because in all seriousness, I believe that the IRS is wonderful. If I'm at a party, and some loud braggart tries to put the IRS down, I brandish my hors d'oeuvre at that person with barely controlled fury and say: "Listen, my friend, if you think you can insult a fine federal agency, which under the bold leadership of

Commissioner Charles O. Rossotti has made big strides toward modernization and improved customer service, then be prepared to take a celery stalk to the eyeball."

Call me a loyal taxpayer if you want but, gosh darn it, that is how I feel about the IRS.

Anyway, as I say, over the years I have written quite a few columns affectionately "joshing" the IRS. I had planned to do such a column this year, featuring some good-natured "zingers." For example, I was going to suggest that all taxpayers should take a special "tax pardon," under which you would deduct the first $48 million you owed the government, on the grounds that, hey, if Marc Rich doesn't have to pay it, why the heck should YOU? Ha ha! I bet the IRS would get a "kick" out of that!

I was also going to suggest that all you taxpayers check out the fun IRS Internet site that is supposed to teach young people why we pay taxes (**www.irs.gov/individuals/page/0,,id=15567,00.html**). This site features cartoon characters such as "Sherri Shine" and "PJ Fly," who speak in "hep" youthful slang lingo, as when Sherri Shine says, "So, like, who invented this tax thing?"

On the IRS site, you travel through history with Sherri and PJ in PJ's "time taxi" and learn everything about the American tax system, except (1) why it's riddled with loopholes for special interests; and (2) why it's incomprehensible to most Americans. At the end of this journey, you realize, along with Sherri and PJ, that we have a really swell and fair tax system, and that we need to pay taxes so our government can provide us with benefits such as . . . well, such as an elaborate Internet site that brainwashes young people.

Ha ha! There I go again! What a kidder I am!

So these were some of the humorous "digs" I had planned to take at the IRS this year in my annual tax column. But then, on the VERY MORNING that I was going to write this column, an amazing coincidence occurred: *I got a letter from the IRS, informing me that I have been chosen for an audit.* I swear I am not making this up. This letter does not have the same fun tone as the IRS Internet site. As I understand it, as a layperson, it basically states that the IRS wants me to produce every document that has ever existed, including the original Magna Carta.

I admit that, for just a moment, I wondered if maybe I was being audited because I have written so many columns "poking fun" at the IRS. But then I thought: No way! Because the fine folks of the IRS have a GREAT sense of humor. I'm sure they know that, deep down inside, I am their biggest fan.

That's why this year, instead of my usual "sarcastic" tax column, I want to take this opportunity to sincerely express how much I love the IRS. I am CRAZY for the IRS. I want to kiss the IRS on the lips. I want to take the IRS to a drive-in movie and make a serious move in the direction of third base. That is the passion I feel for the IRS and its director, Mr. Rossotti, who is a god among men. Mr. Rossotti, if you are reading this, let me say in all sincerity that it would be my personal honor to clean your insoles with my tongue. Thank you for even considering this offer.

And to you taxpayers out there, let me say this: Make sure you file your tax return on time! And remember that, even though income taxes can be a "pain in the neck," the folks at the IRS are regular people just like you, except that they can destroy your life. Also, please send me food in prison.

Daddy's Little Girl
a Republican Barbie

What I do, first thing every morning, is play with dolls. The dolls belong to my fifteen-month-old daughter, Sophie, who likes to start the day by giving her dolls a toy bottle. She has a strong nurturing instinct, although it is not matched by her hand-eye coordination, so often she sticks the bottle into a doll's eye. The dolls don't mind. They're always happy. They talk in perky, squeaky doll voices.

"Hi, Sophie!" say the dolls. "Cough cough cough!"

The dolls cough a lot, because I provide their voices, and it is not easy to sound perky and squeaky when you're a fifty-three-year-old man and it is 7 A.M. and you have not had your coffee. You have to struggle to get yourself into a doll-voice mood, and you find yourself wondering what all the other fifty-three-year-old men are doing at that hour. You suspect they're doing manly, grown-up things, like baling hay, or preparing a sales presentation, or burping. They're probably not lying on the family-room floor, speaking for a Barbie doll.

Yes, my daughter has a Barbie doll. And not just any Barbie doll: It's a Republican Convention Delegate Barbie. Really. She's wearing a business suit and has a little delegate credential around her neck. In other respects she's a regular Barbie, by which I mean she has an anatomically impossible figure and enough hair to be a fire hazard.

Republican Convention Delegate Barbie was given to my daughter by a woman I know who is connected with the Mattel company, which made a limited number of Republican and Democratic Barbies that were given to the delegates last year at both political conventions. The woman told me that Convention Delegate Barbie is a valuable collectible item, and we should keep her in the box. But of course as soon as Sophie saw Barbie, she had to get her out of the box and give her a nice, nurturing bottle to the eyeball.

For some reason, Sophie also likes to undress this Barbie, the result being that she (Barbie) can often be found lying among the other toys on the family-room floor, largely naked, her big hairdo going in all directions, as though she has just been engaging in wild party activities with Elmo and Winnie the Pooh, who lie nearby, looking happy but tired. I suspect that, when I am not looking, they smoke little toy cigarettes.

In case you were wondering (and you know you were): Republican Convention Delegate Barbie does not wear a brassiere. I will not go into details here, except to say that if real Republican convention delegates looked like this Barbie, Bill Clinton would definitely have changed parties.

Anyway, I don't mind playing dolls with Sophie, but it has been an adjustment for me. When my son, Rob, was that age, he played exclusively with trucks, so when I played with him in the morning, all I had to do was make a truck sound, BRRRMMM, which was virtually identical to snoring. And before you accuse me of giving my children gender-stereotyped toys, let me stress that I got Sophie a truck, a big studly one. She uses it as a baby carriage. Sometimes she gives it a bottle.

When we're done playing dolls, it's time for Sophie's other favorite activity: watching the same videotape 850 times. As you parents know, babies LOVE repetition. If babies went to comedy clubs, a successful comedian's routine would go like this:

COMEDIAN: I just flew in from the coast, and boy are my arms tired!

AUDIENCE: (Wild laughter.)

COMEDIAN: I just flew in from the coast, and boy are my arms tired!

AUDIENCE: (Wild laughter.)

COMEDIAN: I just flew in from the coast, and . . .

And so on. Lately, the video we watch 850 times a day is "Baby Bach," in which video images of toys are accompanied by classical music. The theory behind this video, as I understand it, is that looking at these images, and listening to Bach, makes the baby more intelligent. That may be, but it also slowly drives the parents insane. One day, you're going to read a news story about a person who went berserk with a machine gun in a shopping mall when the public-address system started playing classical music. When police search that person's house, I guarantee you they will find "Baby Bach."

But so WHAT if I'm going crazy? The important thing is, Sophie is learning! She's getting smarter by the minute!

She just stuck a bottle in my eye.

Onward, Upward Go the Sherpa and Schlepper

You can imagine my reaction when I found out that Jamling Tenzing Norgay was coming to Miami.

My reaction was: "Who?"

Then I found out that he is the son of Tenzing Norgay, the legendary Sherpa guide who was with Edmund Hillary in 1953 when they became the first people to reach the top of Mount Everest. In 1996, Jamling followed in his father's footsteps as the climbing leader of the team that went to the summit and filmed the IMAX movie *Everest*. He was coming to Miami to talk about his excellent book on that expedition, *Touching My Father's Soul*.

In other words, a world-class mountain climber — a man who survived one of the deadliest climbs on earth — was coming to my city. Not to brag, but I am something of a climber myself. On several occasions, at risk of personal discomfort, I have bypassed a hotel elevator and ascended to the mezzanine level via the stairs.

So I wanted to climb something with Jamling Tenzing Norgay. Specifically, I wanted to climb the highest mountain in Miami-Dade County. I knew this would not be easy, because there ARE no mountains in Miami-Dade County. All of South Florida is basically at sea level, which is why every time there's a hurricane, we wind up with ocean-dwelling fish in our family rooms, flopping around and moving their mouths as if to say: "What are YOU doing here, Lung Breath? This is SEA LEVEL!"

So I decided that, in lieu of a mountain, Jamling and I would attempt to climb the closest approximation we have: The South Dade Solid Waste Disposal Facility. This is a South Florida landmark, known locally as "Mount Trashmore." It's basically a large mound of garbage covered with dirt.

I proposed this climb to Jamling through his publisher. He agreed to do it, partly because he is a brave man who relishes a challenge, but mainly because he was on a book tour. When you've been on a book tour for a while, you give up and do whatever anybody asks you to do. When I'm on book tour, I allow TV makeup people to apply so much mascara to me that I become a dead ringer for Elizabeth Taylor.

And so on a Saturday morning, I met up with Jamling, a quiet and dignified man, and together we attempted to summit Mount Trashmore. I will not ruin the suspense by telling you up front whether we died. Instead, I will give you a dramatic, minute-by-minute account:

9 A.M. — We set out. Almost immediately I consider turning back, because it is terrifying. I'm referring here to the South Florida traffic, where the motto is: "GET OUT OF MY WAY! CAN'T YOU SEE I'M ON MY CELLPHONE?!?"

9:30 A.M. — We arrive at Mount Trashmore, where we meet our guides for the ascent: communications director Gayle Love, and Bill Thorne, whose title is "chief of landfills." We discuss the ascent, and agree that if spoken communication becomes difficult on the summit, we will use hand signals. For example, waving your hand would indicate "Hi!"

9:38 A.M. — Nothing dramatic happens during this particular minute.

9:40 A.M. — We start our ascent. It is frankly easier than I expected. This is because we are riding up in a Jeep. I wonder why this technique has not been used to ascend Everest, but do not mention it to Jamling, lest he smack his forehead and say, "NOW you tell me!"

9:43 A.M. — We're almost to the top, a place where few humans have ever been, unless you count the several hundred people who drive dump trucks up there daily. We leave the Jeep and walk to the summit, ascending a slope that is pitched at about the same angle as a shuffleboard court. That is the kind of mountaineering studs we are.

9:45 A.M. — The summit! We stand 149 feet above sea level, just 28,879 feet lower than Mount Everest itself. It does not smell nearly as bad as we expected. I ask Jamling to compare this experience with being atop Everest.

"It's very different," he says.

10 A.M. — We begin our descent. On the way down, Chief of Landfills Thorne informs us that Mount Trashmore contains — I am not making this up — human body parts AND dead whales. I can tell Jamling is impressed.

10:03 A.M. — We reach sea level, tired but proud. On the way back to the hotel, we are killed in a car crash.

No, really, we got back fine. It was a successful expedition, and Jamling was a great sport. So buy his book, okay? Because it's there.

Considerate Guests Use
the Gas Station Bathroom

I received a letter from a reader named Dick Demers, who relates a shocking story:

It seems Dick and his wife had driven a long distance to visit his wife's sister. Wishing to refresh himself, Dick went into the guest bathroom, took a shower, then dried himself off.

That's the story. Pretty shocking, huh?

Dick's wife thought so. She was horrified.

"You used the GOOD TOWELS!" she said.

And he had. It's a mistake many guys make. A guy will be in a guest bathroom, dripping wet, and he sees a towel, and for some insane reason he thinks it was put there for guests to dry themselves with.

In fact, as Dick's wife angrily pointed out to him, the towels they were supposed to use were NOT in the bathroom; they were (of course!) in the bedroom. The towel Dick used was intended solely as decoration.

Here's a similar bonehead error that guys often commit in guest bathrooms: They see soap on a soap dish, and they use it to *wash their hands*. This of course ruins the guest soap, which is defined as "soap that guests are not supposed to use." Its purpose is to match the guest towels.

In his letter to me, Dick criticized this kind of thinking by comparing it to a hypothetical situation involving guys. Suppose, he wrote, that a guy is working on his car, and he asks you to hand him a $9/16$ wrench. You go over to some wrenches hanging on the wall, and you start to take one, and the guy yells, "NOT THOSE! THOSE ARE FOR DECORATION!"

Dick, when you put it that way, the concept of purely decorative towels DOES seem silly. But there's actually a very logical explanation for it: Women are insane.

No, I am of course just kidding. There really is a good reason. I just don't know what it is. What I do know is that the practice of providing guests with conveniences they cannot use is not limited to the bathroom. The guest bedroom is usually equipped with decorative candles that you must not burn, because that would ruin them. Also you must never throw any waste into the decorative wastebasket, which has never contained any waste and may have been waxed just prior to your arrival. If, during your visit, you generate waste, you should hide it in your suitcase and take it home.

But the trickiest thing is the guest bed. Oh, it may have attractive pillows on it, and a comfy-looking quilt, but you are NOT supposed to use these. You're supposed to take the pillows — which are called "shams" — off the bed and replace them with the *real* pillows, which are hidden somewhere, generally in the closet, which is where you're supposed to put the quilt, which is on the bed solely to match the shams and should NOT come into contact with your disgusting, oily guest body.

If your hostess subscribes to *Martha Stewart Living*, the guest bed may be so massively fortified with decorative objects that it can be deconstructed for sleeping use only by a licensed interior designer. I'm talking about a bed that is surrounded by a dust ruffle and buried under a complex, towering arrangement of approximately forty-six shams and other decorative pillows, which are on top of the quilt, which may be encased in a "duvet cover" and further accessorized by (these are real decorator names) a "soutache." In extreme cases, the entire bed will be surrounded by a giant net, as if to protect it from vampire bats (which will be dyed to match the duvet cover).

If you, as a guest, encounter such a bed, do NOT approach it. Back slowly out of the room, and sleep on the lawn.

Of course, you won't encounter these problems if you're a guest in a household run by a guy, because he won't have fancy guest bedding. In fact, he won't have a guest bed. You'll sleep on the sofa under a Batman beach towel with stains dating back to the Reagan administration. In the morning, you can use this towel to dry yourself after your shower. Feel free to use the guest soap, which you can assemble yourself from ancient shards of Dial on the shower floor.

But to get back to Dick Demers's letter: Dick, you make a logical point about the towels. But this is not about logic; this is about etiquette, and too often we males forget the basic underlying principle of all etiquette, which is: We are scum. So I urge you to apologize to your wife's sister, and henceforth show proper respect for her good towels by not treating them as if they were towels.

And do NOT blow your nose on the shams.

Ban Cellphones — Unless You're Attacked by a Giant Squid

It was a beautiful day at the beach — blue sky, gentle breeze, calm sea. I knew these things because a man sitting five feet from me was shouting them into his cellular telephone, like a play-by-play announcer.

"IT'S A BEAUTIFUL DAY," he shouted. "THE SKY IS BLUE, AND THERE'S A BREEZE, AND THE WATER IS CALM, AND . . ."

Behind me, a woman, her cellphone pressed to her ear, was pacing back and forth.

"She DIDN'T," she was saying. "No. She DIDN'T. She DID? Really? Are you SERIOUS? She did NOT. She DID? No, she DIDN'T. She DID? NO, she . . ."

And so on. This woman had two children, who were frolicking in the surf. I found myself watching them, because the woman surely was not. A giant squid could have surfaced and snatched the children, and this woman would not have noticed. Or, if she had noticed, she'd have said, "Listen, I have to go, because a giant squid just . . . No! She didn't! She DID? No! She . . ."

And next to me, the play-by-play man would have said: ". . . AND A GIANT SQUID JUST ATE TWO CHILDREN, AND I'M GETTING A LITTLE SUNBURNED, AND . . ."

It used to be that the major annoyance at the beach was the jerk who brought a boom box and cranked it up so loud that the bass notes caused seagulls to explode. But at least you knew where these jerks were; you never know which beachgoers have cellphones. You'll settle next to what appears to be a sleeping sunbather, or even (you hope) a corpse, and you'll sprawl happily on your towel, and you'll get all the way to the second sentence of your 467-page book before you doze off to the hypnotic surge of the surf, and . . .

BREEP! BREEP! The corpse sits up, gropes urgently for its cellphone, and shouts, "Hello! Oh hi! I'm at the beach! Yes! The beach! Yes! It's nice! Very peaceful! Very relaxing! What? She did? No, she didn't! She DID? No, she . . ."

Loud cell-phoners never seem to get urgent calls. Just once, I'd like to hear one of them say: "Hello? Yes, this is Dr. Johnson. Oh, hello, Dr. Smith. You've opened the abdominal cavity? Good! Now the appendix should be right under the . . . What? No, that's the liver. Don't take THAT out, ha ha! Oh, you did? Whoops! Okay, now listen very, very carefully . . ."

The good news is, some politicians want to ban cellphone use. The bad news is, they want to ban it in cars, which is the one place where innocent bystanders don't have to listen to it. Granted, drivers using cellphones may cause accidents ("I gotta go, because I just ran over a man, and he's bleeding from the . . . What? She DID? NO, she didn't. She DID? No, she . . ."). But I frankly don't believe that drivers yakking on cellphones are nearly as dangerous as drivers with babies in the backseat. I'm one of those drivers, and we're definitely a menace, especially when our baby has dropped her Elmo doll and is screaming to get it back, and we're steering with one hand while groping under the backseat with the other. ("Groping for Elmo" would be a good name for a rock band.)

So we should, as a long-overdue safety

measure, ban babies. But that is not my point. My point is that there is good news on the cellphone front, which is that several companies — including Image Sensing Systems and Netline — are selling devices that jam cellphone signals. Yes! These devices broadcast a signal that causes every cellphone in the immediate vicinity to play the 1974 hit song "Kung Fu Fighting."

No, that would be too wonderful. But, really, these devices, which start at around $900, cause all nearby cellular phones to register NO SERVICE.

Unfortunately, there's a catch. Because of some outfit calling itself the "Federal Communications Commission," the cellphone jamming devices are illegal in the United States. I say this stinks. I say we should all contact our congresspersons and tell them that if they want to make it up to us consumers for foisting those lousy low-flow toilets on us, they should put down their interns for a minute and pass a law legalizing these devices, at least for beach use.

I realize some of you disagree with me. I realize you have solid reasons — perhaps life-and-death reasons — why you MUST have your cellular phone working at all times, everywhere. If you're one of those people, please believe me when I say this: I can't hear you.

Quality! Craftsmanship!
Service Contract!

Recently I was in an electronics store, trying to buy a telephone that was just a telephone. I did not want the conference-call feature, the intercom feature, the programmable memory feature, the coffee-making feature, or the feature (this is a new one) that displays the exact current latitude and longitude of Rep. Gary Condit. All I wanted was the feature that lets you talk to the person on the other end.

After much searching, I found a phone — probably manufactured during the Spanish-American War — that hardly did anything. ("Hardly Does Anything!" would be an excellent product slogan, if you ask me.) While I was looking at this phone, a previously invisible salesperson materialized next to me and said the words that I have come to detest more than any others in the English language except "prostate exam."

Those words are: "You definitely should

get the service agreement."

In case you just got here from the Lost Continent of Atlantis, let me explain the service-agreement concept: When you buy a product, you pay extra money to the store, and the store gives you a piece of paper. This gives you, the consumer, the peace of mind that comes from knowing that if, for any reason, at any time, something goes wrong with your product, you will not be able to find the service agreement. Most likely you won't even remember you bought it. Your brain will be clogged with too much other information, such as how to work the intercom feature.

Stores LOVE service agreements, for the same reason you'd love to have money fall on you from the sky. As a result, when you buy a product today, you get this bizarre multiple-personality sales pitch, because at the same time that the salesperson is telling you how swell the product is, he's suggesting it will need a LOT of service:

SALESPERSON: . . . so this is an excellent product. Totally reliable.

YOU: I'll take it!

SALESPERSON: It's going to break.

YOU: What?

SALESPERSON: There's this thing

inside? The confabulator? You're lucky if that baby lasts you a week.

YOU: So you're saying it's NOT a good product?

SALESPERSON: No! It's top of the line! Totally dependable!

YOU: Well, okay, then, I guess I'll . . .

SALESPERSON: Of course if the refrenestator module blows, you're looking at a $263,000 repair, plus parts and labor. One customer had to sell a lung.

In some stores, selling you a product seems to be merely an excuse to sell you the service agreement. Several months ago, my wife and I were shopping for a computer, and a salesperson attached himself to us, lamprey-like. His sole professional contribution was to inform us, no matter which computer we looked at, that we would definitely want the service agreement. At one point he took me aside and told me, Man to Man, that we *especially* needed the service agreement, because — this is a direct quote — "You know how women can be with computers." He did not elaborate, but the implication was that, as soon as a woman is alone with a computer, she has some kind of massive hormonal surge that causes her to, I don't know, lactate on the keyboard.

We did not get that service agreement. Nor did I get the service agreement for the cheap telephone that hardly did anything. In each case, after I said "no" for maybe the fifth time, the salesperson backed slowly away, giving me a look of pity mixed with apprehension, as if the product, unprotected by a service agreement, was going to explode at any moment.

It's only a matter of time before we see stores that have no products at all, just empty aisles prowled by salespersons who glom onto you and relentlessly hector you until you buy a service agreement. Think of the profit margin.

In closing, let me stress that this column is in no way intended to be critical of the retail community, especially the many fine retailers who advertise in this newspaper. If you are such a retailer, and you are for any reason unhappy with anything I've said, simply write me a letter explaining the problem. I'll be happy to correct it!

Be sure to enclose your service agreement.

At 17 (Months),
Her Music Tastes
Match Dad's

You will die of jealousy when I tell you whom I recently saw live in concert: The Bear in the Big Blue House.

For those of you who do not have small children, let me explain that The Bear in the Big Blue House is a major morning-TV star. I'd go so far as to say that, with his talent, some day he could be as big as Elmo. We watch his show every morning while we're feeding our seventeen-month-old daughter, Sophie, her breakfast, by which I mean picking her food off the floor and checking to see if it's still clean enough to eat.

I like the Bear's show because it meets the single most important artistic criterion for children's TV: It is not Barney. I hate Barney, because he is a large annoying purple wad of cuteness, and his songs are lame, and some of the "children" on the show appear to be in their mid-twenties. They are definitely too old to skip, and yet they skip everywhere. They must have a mandatory skipping clause in their contracts, because it is their only mode of transport. If they were in a burning building, they would skip to the exits. I suspect that when they finish taping the *Barney* show, they skip behind the studio and drink gin.

On *The Bear in the Big Blue House*, there are no children, only animals, the main one being the Bear, which I assume is a guy wearing a bear suit, although it moves in a realistic manner, so it could be an actual bear wearing a bear suit. The Bear has various animal friends, which are played by people's hands inside puppets. (DISCUSSION QUESTION: Do the hands wear the puppets when they rehearse? Or is the rehearsal just a bunch of naked hands talking to each other?)

Anyway, one morning we were reading the newspaper and picking Sophie's food off the floor, and suddenly my wife said: "The Bear is going to give a live concert in Miami!"

"The Bear in the BIG BLUE HOUSE??" I said.

"Yes!" she said, and we both became

more excited than when the Berlin Wall fell. This gives you an idea how pathetic it is to be the parent of a small child.

Of course we got tickets to the show, which was also attended by, at a conservative estimate, every small child in the western hemisphere. There has probably never been an event where more audience members were wearing diapers, other than a Tom Jones concert.

The Bear's show was excellent by any artistic standard, except the standard of being able to actually hear it. That was because at any given moment, at least a third of the audience was crying. Fortunately, Sophie was in a good mood: She stood on our laps for the whole show, clapping and shouting "Yayyyy!" in response to everything that happened, including the announcement that flash photographs were prohibited.

Despite the audience noise level, it was possible, if you listened hard, to follow the program. It opened with one of the Bear's hit songs "What's That Smell?"

"Hey!" I shouted to my wife. "He's singing 'What's That Smell?'!" We sang along, as did many other parents. Meanwhile, all over the theater, youngsters responded to the song by shouting, shrieking, falling down, running away, crying, babbling, rolling on the floor, sleeping, gurgling, burping, and going to the bathroom. At the end of the song, Sophie clapped her hands and went "Yayyyy!" This was the basic procedure for all the rest of the songs.

During the intermission, vendors came into the theater to sell — I swear — helium balloons. Many children got them, which meant that the audience, in addition to not being able to hear, could not see. Nevertheless, we parents continued to sing along to such hit songs as "Magic in the Kitchen," "The Bear Cha Cha Cha" and my personal favorite, "Otter Love Rap," a hip-hop style of song that explores the too-often-ignored topic of otters who love, and the otters who love them. I don't mind saying that I was "getting down" to that particular song, and so was Sophie, to judge from her comment when it ended ("Yayyyy!").

It was a fine father-daughter moment, made only slightly bittersweet by the knowledge that, soon enough, Sophie will want to go to concerts by some synthetic prefabricated soul-free "boy band." She'll want me to drop her off out front of the concert and then disappear, lest I embarrass her in front of her friends by the mere fact of my existence. But for now, for a little while, I'm as cool as anybody she knows. Yayyyy.

He's Got a Broom
and He's Not Afraid
to Use It

A very important issue that we all need to be concerned about is global warming, and we will get to that shortly, but first we need to discuss the issue of what happened the other night in my kitchen.

It began when I was in the bedroom, flossing my teeth (I keep my teeth in the bedroom). Suddenly my wife, who is not normally a burster, burst in and said: "There's a bat in the kitchen!"

A good snappy comeback line would have been: "No thanks! I already ate!" But snappy comebacks are not what is called for in this type of situation. What is called for, by tradition, is for The Man of the House to put down his dental floss and go face the bat.

So I went to the kitchen, passing en route through the living room, where my wife and her mother, who was visiting us, were huddled together, protecting each other. Neither one made a move to protect ME, the person going to his doom.

I opened the kitchen door and peeked inside, and, sure enough, there was a large black thing flitting around, banging itself against the ceiling. This was a perfect example of why — no matter what you hear from the liberal communist news media — private citizens have a legitimate constitutional need for machine guns. No single-shot weapon is going to bring down a flitting bat in a kitchen at close range. To stop one of those babies, you need to put a LOT of lead into the air. Yes, innocent appliances could get hurt. But that is the price of freedom.

Unfortunately, the only weapon I had was a broom. And to get it, I had to get to the other side of the kitchen, which meant going *directly under the bat.* You know how, in John Wayne war movies, when it's time to go into battle, John Wayne gives out a mighty whoop and charges boldly forward with his head held high? Well, that is not how I crossed the kitchen. I scooted with tiny mincing steps, hunched over, emitting a series of high-pitched whimpers designed to assure the bat that not only was I harmless, but I was also willing, if necessary, to bear its young.

Reaching the other side, I grabbed the broom and turned to face the bat, at which point I made a shocking discovery: *The bat was a butterfly.* It was totally black, except that it had, I swear, red eyes, which were GLOWING. I realize that you may not believe me, so at this point I am going to bring in a trusted American icon to corroborate my story.

ABRAHAM LINCOLN: Dave is telling the truth. It was a large black butterfly, and it had glowing red eyes.

When Abraham Lincoln and I say that this butterfly was "large," we are not whistling "Dixie." This was by FAR the largest butterfly I have ever encountered. Are you familiar with the 1961 Japanese movie *Mothra*, in which downtown Tokyo is attacked by a 230-foot-long, 20,000-ton moth, played by the late Ethel Merman? Well, the butterfly in my kitchen could have used Mothra as an ear plug. (Assuming that butterflies have ears.)

So anyway, when I saw that the bat was, in fact, a butterfly, I knew exactly what to do. Specifically, I yelled: "It's a butterfly!" This was for the benefit of my wife. I'm sure the butterfly already knew it was a butterfly.

"Oh! Then don't harm it!" answered my wife, in an alternate universe. In the present universe, she answered, "Well, KILL IT!" Women have a reputation for being gentle and nurturing, but in my experience, they pretty much want to wipe out every creature on the Great Tree of Life below the level of poodle.

So there, alone in the kitchen, armed only with a broom, I went head-to-head with the Giant Demon Butterfly from Hell. It clearly was not afraid of me. It flitted right at me in the aggressive, confident manner of a creature that, in the wild, preys on wolverines.

How well did I handle myself? I certainly don't want to toot my own horn.

ABRAHAM LINCOLN: Dave was very, very brave.

In the end, I broke the broom, but I also sent the butterfly to that Big Cocoon in the Sky. So now our house is quiet again. But I am uneasy. I find myself wondering: Where did that thing COME from? What if there's ANOTHER one out there?

I frankly don't know how anyone can think about global warming at a time like this.

There's No Denying
Nature's Wake-up Call

A man — we'll call him "Harvey" — went to see a doctor, complaining of tiredness, bruises all over his body, shooting pains, and quotation marks around his name. The doctor immediately recognized these symptoms: "Harvey" had a snoring problem. At night, he was being jabbed repeatedly by his wife, trying to make him shut up. Also, somebody had apparently been shooting him.

Yes, snoring is a serious health problem, one that affects more Americans than shark attacks and Rep. Gary Condit *combined*. Yet many people — and here I am in no way referring to my wife — refuse to admit that they snore. Even if they routinely emit nocturnal noises that cause shingles to fly off the roof, they will be outraged that you would leap to the conclusion that they are the source of the snoring, without considering other explanations, such as that a third party, unknown to either of you, is sleeping in your bed.

Women — and once again I am NOT referring to my wife — tend to be the worst snoring-deniers, because women are taught from an early age that it is not feminine to emit any noise or aroma that would indicate that they are biological organisms. Men, on the other hand, consider bodily functions to be a highly masculine form of manliness. That's why men are not afraid to haul off and let go of a hearty burp, often as a way to emphasize a rhetorical point (Four score and seven BWOOOOOOOOOOOORP years ago . . .).

Men also take pride in another, even more basic, bodily emission, which, because this is a family newspaper, I will refer to by its technical name, "making a tooter." This is a popular thing to do whenever males gather together. As a youth, I was a Boy Scout, and while I know that scouting is a fine activity that has taught countless young men important leadership and character-building skills, the major activity in my particular troop was slicing the Muenster. We'd go on a camping trip, and for dinner we'd consume huge quantities of Campbell's brand Pork 'n' Mainly Beans, and by nightfall the hills were alive with the sound of tooting. Eventually the entire area would be blanketed by a giant mushroom cloud of Boy Scout gas that caused flocks of migrating geese to reverse course ("Turn back! We're spending the winter in Canada!").

Medical science tells us that, one way or another, the average man releases 6,000 metric quarts of gas per day, and significantly more if he is in an elevator. Meanwhile, the average woman, striving to be feminine, is keeping all that gas bottled up *inside her body*. This results in an enormous pressure buildup that can, later in life, cause an explosive and embarrassing medical condition known as "The Mount Vesuvius Syndrome." This is precisely why one well-known woman — who, out of respect for her privacy, I will refer to here only as "The Queen of England" — is accompanied at all times by men with bagpipes.

At this point, it might be a good idea for all of us to go back to the beginning of this column to see what our topic is. Okay, there it is, snoring. As I was saying, most of us snore, even though — and I am STILL not in any way referring to my wife — we refuse to admit it.

But what is snoring? Medically, it is

when air has trouble getting past the uvula, which is a part of your body that sounds like a dirty word but is actually not. You are free to say it in polite company, in sentences such as: "I hear Todd has a huge uvula."

How serious is snoring? To answer that question, I consulted my colleague Gene Weingarten, who happens to be one of the nation's most respected hypochondriacs. Gene is the author of an excellent book, *The Hypochondriac's Guide to Life and Death*, which has a chapter entitled "Hiccups Can Mean Cancer."

Needless to say, Gene's opinion is that snoring can, and probably does, indicate a seriously fatal problem. The good news, he told me, is that snoring can be cured by a surgical procedure "that basically shears off the entire back of your throat." Gene adds: "It doesn't always solve the problem."

But what do you care? YOU don't snore.

Grab Your Pajamas, It's World Series Time

This is the time of year when Americans make a sincere effort to care about the World Series, which determines which baseball team will be the champion of the entire world, except for the part of the world located outside the United States and southeastern Canada.

But the heck with that part. This is OUR national pastime, and that's why the World Series arouses our passion, even if we stopped paying attention to pro baseball some years ago, when it started adding mutant teams with names like the Tampa Bay Area Fighting Seaweeds.

Why is baseball our national pastime? Because it is a metaphor for life itself. As George Will put it: "In life, as in baseball, we must leave the dugout of complacency, step up to the home plate of opportunity, adjust the protective groin cup of caution, and swing the bat of hope at the curve ball of fate, hoping that we can hit a line drive of success past the shortstop of misfortune, then sprint down the basepath of chance, knowing that at any moment we may pull the hamstring muscle of inadequacy and fall face-first onto the field of failure, where the chinch bugs of broken dreams will crawl into our nose."

Yes, baseball is very deep, although this is not obvious from looking at it. If you don't grasp the nuances, baseball appears to be a group of large, unshaven men standing around in their pajamas and frowning, as if thinking: "My arms are so big that I can no longer groom myself!" Yet show the same scene to serious baseball fans, and they will see a complex, fascinating, almost artistic tableau. Why? Because they have consumed huge quantities of the drug "Ecstasy."

No, seriously, it's because these fans appreciate the subtleties of baseball. To help you perceive these subtleties during the World Series, here's a quick "refresher course," starting with:

THE ORIGINS OF BASEBALL: Mankind has played games involving sticks and balls for hundreds of thousands of years. Meanwhile, Womankind had her hands full raising Childrenkind, but whenever she asked Mankind to lend a hand, he'd answer, "Not now! We have a no-hitter going!" That was true, because numbers had not been invented yet.

Then, in 1839, along came a man named Abner Doubleday, who as you can imagine took a lot of ribbing because his name could be rearranged to spell not only "A Barely Nude Bod" but also "Lure Dad By A Bone." Nevertheless, he invented a game that included virtually all of the elements of modern-day baseball, including Bob Costas and the song "Who Let the Dogs Out?" This led to the Civil War.

BASEBALL TODAY: Baseball today is very much the same as it was 150 years ago, except that, for security reasons, the games take place after the public has gone to bed. The rules are simple: Each team sends nine players onto the field, except for one team, which sends one — the "batter" — plus two elderly retired players called "coaches," who constantly touch themselves on various parts of their bodies to communicate, via Secret Code, the message: "Tobacco juice has corroded my brain into a lump of dead tissue the size of a grape."

The object of baseball is for the "pitcher" to throw the "ball" into the "strike zone." This is almost impossible, because the only person who knows the location of the strike zone is the "umpire," and he refuses to reveal it because of a bitter, decades-old labor dispute between his union and Major League Baseball. On any given day, the strike zone may not even be in the stadium; there's simply no way to tell. The umpire communicates solely by making ambiguous hand gestures and shouting something that sounds like "HROOOOT!," which he refuses to explain.

Eventually, the pitcher throws the ball at the batter, in case the strike zone is located somewhere on his body. This is the signal for all the players to run to the middle of the field and engage in a form of combat similar to professional wrestling, except that sometimes professional wrestlers, by accident, actually hit each other. This never happens in baseball, where the last player to land a punch was Babe Ruth, who in the 1921 World Series, knocked out his own self. Instead of punching, baseball players fight by grabbing each other's shirts and exchanging fierce glares, as if to say: "You're gonna get a PERMANENT WRINKLE IN YOUR PAJAMAS, BUSTER!"

After nine "innings" of this, the team

with the most "runs" wins. I don't know how the runs happen, because by then I'm asleep. But I sleep in front of the TV, in a rooting position. My body language clearly says: "I may not know who's playing, but if they don't win, it's a shame."

Burger King Puts Workers' Feet to the Fire — Literally

A while back I read a fascinating business-related article in my newspaper, the *Miami Herald* (official motto: "The Person Who Was Supposed to Think Up Our Motto Got Laid Off"). This article, which was written by Elaine Walker, concerned an incident wherein employees of the Burger King marketing department walked barefoot over hot coals.

If you're unfamiliar with modern American corporate culture, you're probably assuming that somebody spiked the Burger King coffee machine with LSD. Nope. The firewalking was a planned activity on a corporate motivational retreat, supervised by a professional fire-walking consultant to whom Burger King paid thousands of actual U.S. dollars.

According to the *Herald* article, the consultant also had the Burger King marketing people bend spoons, break boards, smash bricks, bend steel bars with their throats, and walk over a bed of sharp nails. American corporate employees are required to do this kind of thing all the time, and for a sound business reason: Their management has lint for brains.

No, seriously, these are motivational activities that make employees self-confident and unafraid to tackle tough business challenges. The employees think: "Hey, if I can bend a steel bar with my throat, there's no reason why I can't change the toner cartridge in the printer!"

The Burger King people got off easy. Some corporations motivate their employees by shipping them off to rugged wilderness survival programs, where they learn vital lessons that help them excel in the business world. Like, if they need to impress an important client, they could use their survival training to, I don't know, catch him a squirrel.

The point is that subjecting employees to physical abuse is a standard corporate motivational technique that has proven, in study after study, to be a highly effective means of transferring money to consultants. Still, you might think that employees would draw the line at walking on hot coals, on the grounds that they could, theoretically, burn their feet. This would seem to be especially obvious to employees of Burger King, a company whose main product is a graphic example of what happens to flesh that is exposed to high temperatures.

Nevertheless, at the Burger King marketing retreat, more than one hundred employees walked across an eight-foot strip of white-hot coals, and — in an inspirational triumph of mind over matter that shows the amazing miracles that the human spirit, when freed of self-doubt, can accomplish — about a dozen of them burned their feet. One woman had to be taken to the hospital. Several people were in wheelchairs the next day.

Now, you may feel that an employee-motivation event that actually injured some employees could not be described as a total success. That is why you are not a marketing executive. The *Herald* article quotes Burger King's vice president of product marketing, Dana Frydman — whose personal feet were among those burned — as saying: "It was a great experience for everyone."

The article also quotes the firewalking consultant, Robert "Cork" Kallen, as saying: "The majority of the people get through it without a nick or a blister. When you see over one hundred people and only ten to fifteen people have blisters, I don't term that unusual. Some people just have incredibly sensitive feet."

There you have the REAL problem: employees with sensitive feet. It's high time that corporations did something about this problem. Here's my proposal: When you apply for a job, at the end of your interview, you would be required to take off your shoes and socks, and the interviewer would snap the bottoms of your feet sharply with a rubber band. For particularly important jobs, the interviewer might staple a document to your insole, to see if you truly have the foot toughness it takes to succeed in the modern corporate environment.

What do you think? I think it's a great idea. In fact, I think I would be an excellent motivational consultant. You can be my first client! Here's what you do: (1) Tear this column out of the newspaper. (2) Wad it into a ball. (3) Insert the ball into your left nostril and jam it in there as far as you can with a pencil. (4) Send me thousands of dollars.

Ha ha! I'm just kidding, of course. I know you're not THAT stupid. Hardly anybody is!

NOTE TO MARKETING EXECUTIVES: I would prefer cash.

A Truly Terrifying Act: Doing the Hokey Pokey for Airport Security

Air travel sure is a big old laundry hamper of fun these days. That's what I was thinking as I was removing my clothing in front of hundreds of people at the Denver airport (which is located in Wyoming).

For some reason, my traveling party had been singled out by the security people for a near-proctological level of scrutiny. This surprised me, because my party consisted of me, my wife, and our twenty-month-old daughter.

I cannot imagine terrorists getting anything done if they were traveling with a baby. Every few steps they'd have to change the baby, feed the baby, snatch lethal objects out of the baby's mouth, etc. They'd have no time for anything else. At the end of the day, they'd be going: "Did you commit the act of terror?" "NO! I was wiping chocolate off her Snow White doll!

I thought YOU were going to commit the act of terror!"

Nevertheless, we were singled out. This meant that while the other travelers — all of whom, frankly, looked suspicious to me — zipped through security, we were ordered off to the side, where a man told me to remove my shoes, belt, and wallet, which he handed to a woman, who, without a word, walked off with them. I was hoping that these were security personnel, as opposed to wallet thieves who had figured out that, these days, air travelers will do anything they are ordered to do ("Okay, Mr. Smith, I'm going to ask you to put your left hand in, take your left hand out, do the Hokey Pokey, and shake it all about").

Next, the man told me to hold my arms out so he could scan me. This meant I had to let go of my pants, which, being beltless, began to slide down, an occurrence that I am sure had been recorded in my Terrorist Suspect Profile on some computer somewhere ("USE EXTREME CAUTION. KNOWN MOONER.")

While I was performing as the World's Oldest Chippendale Dancer, other security people were insisting that my daughter toddle alone through the metal detector. But first they made her give up her Cow Baby doll, so they could put it through the scanner. I imagine the Cow Baby doll got their attention because it looks like a cow, but when you lift up the head, you see it's actually a baby wearing a cow costume. This is clearly suspicious ("LOOKS LIKE COW, BUT ACTUALLY IS BABY").

They finally let us pass, but when we got to our gate, they called out our names — only *our* names — and ordered us to hold out our arms to be scanned again, while all the other passengers looked on, no doubt wondering what kind of lowlife terrorists we were to be lugging around a baby. It was embarrassing, but I have to admit that it gave me the security of knowing that if anything remotely suspicious had occurred on the flight, our fellow passengers would have beaten us senseless with their in-flight dinner rolls.

IRRELEVANT CLOSING ANECDOTE: We were traveling as part of a tour with a rock band called the Rock Bottom Remainders. This is a group of authors who raise money for a literacy charity called America Scores by playing amplified instruments in such a way as to bring audiences to their feet, shouting: "Okay, okay, we'll donate! Stop playing!"

One of our show-stopping songs is "Leader of the Pack," the story of a teenage romance tragically ended by a motorcycle crash. Amy Tan sings this song, and we do a little routine wherein Amy's husband, Lou DeMattei, dresses up as a motorcycle gang member and simulates the crash by diving onto the stage. Lou prides himself on the realism of his dive, and during one show it was so realistic that he broke his collarbone.

So with the song still going on, Lou, the "corpse," was lying on the stage in agony, but the rest of us did not know this. Unfortunately, this was the night when I — Mr. Funny Ha-Ha Humor Man — decided to introduce a new comic element into the act, which was to kick the "corpse" to make sure it was "dead." So I kicked Lou. This was so hilarious that another band member, Stephen King, decided that HE would also kick Lou.

Fortunately, Lou was able to stagger off the stage before his wacky bandmates ruptured his spleen. When the show ended, and we found out that Lou had gone to the hospital, we felt AWFUL, and when we saw him again, we apologized profusely. Lou was very gracious about it.

Although, come to think of it, maybe he was the one who gave our names to the Denver security people.

Owner's Manual Step No. 1: Bang Head Against the Wall

The topic of this column is a recent *Washington Post* story stating that manufacturers of appliances, computers, cars, etc., want to know why Americans don't read their owner's manuals.

WARNING: THIS COLUMN IS INTENDED FOR READING PURPOSES ONLY. DO NOT USE THIS COLUMN AS A TOURNIQUET.

One big reason why consumers don't read manuals is that the typical manual starts out with fifteen to twenty-five pages of warnings, informing you of numerous highly unlikely ways in which you could use the product to injure or kill yourself.

WARNING: DO NOT READ THIS COLUMN WHILE WATERSKIING. DO NOT SET FIRE TO THIS COLUMN IN A ROOM FILLED WITH HYDROGEN.

The typical consumer's reaction to these warnings is: "What kind of moron would do THAT?"

The correct answer to this question is: "A wealthy moron." Because the reason these warnings exist is that somewhere, some time, some consumer with the IQ of a radish actually DID one of these bizarre things, and got a lawyer, and sued, and a jury made up of people whose understanding of economics is based entirely on grocery coupons decided, what the heck, $300 million sounds about right, but let's not tell the judge right away because first we should order a pizza.

So every year there are more huge product-liability awards, and every year manufacturers have to put more warnings in the owner's manuals, and every year the radish-brains come up with newer, more innovative ways to injure themselves. There will come a day when every product you buy will come with an actual living lawyer inside the box, sealed in plastic; as soon as you break the seal, the lawyer will emerge and start preparing your product-liability lawsuit. (This system is feasible because product-liability lawyers are spore-based organisms who can survive for years without air.)

Another reason why consumers don't read manuals is that products today have TOO MANY FEATURES. (I know, I know, I've complained about this before. So sue me.) We — and when I say "we," I am speaking for every human being in the world — do not want a lot of features. In fact, for most products, we really want only two features: the "on" feature, and the "off" feature.

An example of a feature that we do not want is "picture in picture." This feature allows you to watch one channel on most of your TV screen, while another channel appears in a little box in the corner. The salesman always makes a big deal out of "picture in picture," and the manual always devotes pages to how you use it.

Except you don't use it. I have never seen any actual human consumer use the "picture in picture" feature, because (a) nobody remembers how it works; (b) it's annoying to have two pictures on the screen; and (c) it's hard enough to find ONE thing on TV you want to watch.

The third reason why consumers don't read manuals is that many consumers are men, and we men would no more read a manual than we would ask directions, because this would be an admission that the person who wrote the manual has a bigger . . . okay, a bigger grasp of technology than we do. We men would rather hook up our new DVD player in such a way that it ignites the DVDs and shoots them across the room — like small flaming UFOs — than admit that the manual-writer possesses a more manly technological manhood than we do.

And then there are some people who simply do not NEED manuals. I refer here to my son, who, like many young people, can immediately grasp how to operate any technological object, no matter how complex. Give my son fifteen minutes in the space shuttle, and he will figure out not only how to launch it into orbit, but also how to make it play really hideous "hip-hop" music loud enough to shatter passing asteroids. (And please do not tell me that sound does not travel through space. "Hip-hop" music travels through *everything*.)

So what does all this mean? It means that if manufacturers want us to read their manuals, they need to take a few simple, common-sense steps: (1) Deport all the product-liability lawyers to Iraq; (2) Get rid of "picture in picture"; (3) Include nothing in the manual except simple, clear, minimal directions, printed on photographs of tennis star Anna Kournikova naked. These steps will greatly improve consumer knowledge, and reduce unfortunate mishaps. You may now place this column over the wound.

(NOTE TO MANUFACTURERS: Make sure it really IS Anna Kournikova, or you will be sued.)

Cap 'n' Gown? I'll Take the Burger 'n' Fries

And so we are gathered here today — you, the eager members of the Class of 2002, and we, your family members, who will sit on these hard folding chairs until every last eager one of you has picked up a diploma, at which point we will feel as though the entire Riverdance troupe has been stomping on our buttocks.

Because, gosh, there sure are a LOT of you in the Class of 2002! We in the audience are wondering if there is anybody in North America besides us who is NOT graduating today. And although we know this is very exciting for you, the Class of 2002, we are fighting to stay awake.

We have already engaged in the traditional time-passing activities of commencement audiences, such as trying to remember the names of all Seven Dwarfs, and looking through the commencement program for comical graduate names. We have nudged the person sitting next to us and pointed to names like "Konrad A. Klamsucker Jr." and "Vorbanna Free-pitude," and that has given us brief moments of happiness.

But we can only do that for so long, Class of 2002, and now we are feeling the despair that comes over members of a commencement audience when they realize that forty minutes have passed, and the dean is just now starting to hand out diplomas to people whose last names start with "D," and the last name of the lone graduate we actually came to see starts with "W."

We've decided that, if we ever have another child threatening to graduate from college, we're going to have that child's name legally changed to "Aaron A. Aardvark." Yes, the other families in the audience will make fun of it. But their laughter will turn to bitter envy when our child gets his diploma first, and we get up off these folding chairs and head for a restaurant! Ha ha!

We also think it would be nice if commencement programs had interesting articles for the audience to read, or even short works of fiction with appropriate educational themes. ("As Vorbanna walked across the stage, her tassel swaying seductively, Konrad watched her, his sweating hands caressing the smooth hardness of his embossed leatherette diploma cover, and he thought about that unforgettable night when the two of them, for the first time, matriculated.")

Another option would be to show movies during the commencement ceremonies. Wouldn't that be great? While we were waiting for specific graduates to get their diplomas, we could enjoy such classic education-related cinema moments as the scene in *Animal House* where John Belushi imitates a giant pimple by squeezing his cheeks and spewing chewed food out of his mouth. That would surely get a roar of delight and approval from the audience, and whichever graduate happened to be on the stage at that moment would think, "Gosh, they certainly are excited about my bachelor's degree in Business Transportation with a minor in Tire Management!" So everybody would benefit.

Sadly, Class of 2002, we are not yet ready, as a society, for this kind of progressive commencement concept. Because the world is not a perfect place. It is a world filled with malice and evil, a world where, today, none of us is truly safe, even in our homes, from the very real danger that a total stranger will call us up and demand that we change our phone company. It will be up to you, the Class of 2002, to tackle these problems — not only to build a better society for tomorrow, but also to take bold action to correct the injustices of the past, starting by promising to pay your parents back for your college tuition.

Ha ha! That was commencement humor, Class of 2002. Your parents do not expect you to pay them back. All that they expect is that you will go out and find your place in the world. Notice that we say, "the world," as opposed to, "your parents' house." Your parents love you very, very much, Class of 2002, but at this stage in their lives, if they could choose between living with you and living with a Labrador retriever, they quite frankly would go with the Labrador retriever. For one thing, it will not expect them to do its laundry.

In closing, Class of 2002, we would like to leave you with some words of wisdom — words that may mean little to you now, but words that, trust us, you will some day want very much to remember. Those words are: Sleepy, Grumpy, Sneezy,

Happy, Dopey, and two other ones. Thank you, good luck, and we'll meet you at the restaurant.

Fitting Into That Bikini
Is Easy As (Eating) Pie

Ladies: It's time to get in shape for swimsuit season! If you start a program of diet and exercise NOW, in just a few weeks you can shed that extra ten pounds, so when it's time to "hit the beach," you can put on that new bikini with the confidence that comes from knowing that you will immediately take off that new bikini, put on a bathrobe, and spend the rest of the weekend in your bedroom, weeping and eating Häagen-Dazs straight from the container.

Because let's face it, ten pounds is not going to get the job done. Not these days, when the strict bodily standards set by supermodels and top Hollywood stars dictate that no woman is supposed to weigh more than her lipstick.

How do these celebrities stay so impossibly thin? Simple: They have full-time personal trainers, who advise them on nutrition, give them pep talks, and shoot them with tranquilizer darts whenever they try to crawl, on hunger-weakened limbs, toward the packet of rice cakes that constitutes the entire food supply in their 37,000-square-foot mansions. For most celebrities, the biggest meal of the day is toothpaste (they use reduced-fat Crest).

But you don't have a personal trainer, which means you have to rely on will-power. And of course you don't HAVE any willpower. If you did, you'd be doing stomach crunches right now, instead of reading this worthless column. But there you sit, lumplike, while the millions of fat cells in your thighs mate furiously and give birth to gigantic litters.

Perhaps you are thinking: "But the super-thin look is out! The fashion industry recently declared that larger sizes were fashionable! Even *Vogue* magazine ran a photo spread wherein some of the models were normal human females!"

No offense, but: You moron. This is a TRICK, a prank that the fashion industry plays every few years. It causes millions of normal-sized women to go to the chic clothing stores, looking to buy the clothes they see in *Vogue*, only to discover that the fashion industry makes these clothes only for mutant women who wear size zero or lower.

"I'm sorry, but we don't have that in your size," you will be told by the snotty seventy-eight-pound salesperson, who enters and leaves the store via the mail slot. "You might try across the street, at Big Betty's Duds for Whales."

So what CAN you ladies do to prepare for swimsuit season? You can do what we men have been doing, with great success, for so many years: nothing. Most of us men have no problem parading around the beach in a bathing suit, even if it reveals that we have enough spare belly tissue to create a whole new person. What is our secret? Why are we so secure about our bodies? Simple: *We have no idea what our bodies look like.*

This is because of the way we use mirrors. Most women check out their body from all angles, in this order: (1) front, (2) side, (3) back. Naturally, the last two views are the ones they remember best, and over time they come to see themselves as consisting almost entirely of a stomach and a butt.

Most men, on the other hand, never look at anything but the front view, which is the most flattering. I'm a perfect example. For decades, having looked at myself only head-on, I thought I had a normal nose. It wasn't until I reached my forties that I realized, after seeing explicit photographs of my profile, that my face is dominated by a glob of nasal flesh the size and shape of a mature Bartlett pear.

So now I make a conscious effort to keep my head pointed directly toward people, so they can't see my profile. If I have a passenger in my car, I drive using peripheral vision, which means I may run over the occasional person on the sidewalk, or even inside a building. But at least my passenger thinks I have a normal nose.

You ladies can use a similar technique for swimwear. Your role model should be the football defensive back. When the receiver goes out for a pass, the defensive back stays right with him, but runs backward and sideways, so he is always facing the receiver. It looks as though the defensive back is extremely self-conscious about the size of his booty. Study this technique, ladies, and use it at the beach! If your footwork is solid, nobody will ever see anything but a flattering, head-on view. If you suffer a knee injury, try to fall so that your back is on the sand. If you need surgery, demand sugar-free anesthetic. And above all: Have a great summer!

Don't Mean a Thing
If It Ain't Got That Swing

You don't think of swingers as being the type of people who hold conventions. By "swingers," I mean couples who swing with other couples. By "swing," I mean, "you know exactly what I mean."

But my point is that you (and by "you," I mean "I") don't think of swingers as being big conventiongoers. You think of them as hanging out at private parties, or exclusive swinger nightclubs, or secluded motels, or the Clinton White House. You don't picture swingers walking around large convention hotels wearing name badges and attending seminars, like executives in the forklift industry.

But it turns out that swingers do hold conventions. I know this because I went to one recently, at the Radisson Deauville Hotel in Miami Beach. I was accompanied by my wife and a guy named Wally, who's in the insurance business.

This was not as kinky as it sounds. Wally

had been the highest bidder in a charity auction for a lunch with me. He assumed we would be going to a normal restaurant where everybody would be wearing clothes. But when I suggested to him that we could use the lunch as an opportunity to investigate — for journalism purposes — the swingers' convention, he readily agreed, despite the very real risk that we might see people, including women, wearing skimpy or nonexistent outfits. That is the kind of sacrifice some guys are willing to make for charity.

I also invited my wife to go along, so that I would not be walking into a swingers' convention accompanied only by an insurance executive named Wally. When I invited her, I made a hilarious joke, strictly kidding around in a humorous vein, about how maybe we would find a couple we'd want to swap with.

NOTE TO HUSBANDS: Never attempt to make this type of joke with your wife. This type of joke should be attempted only by trained humor professionals.

NOTE TO TRAINED HUMOR PROFESSIONALS: Even then, it turns out to be a bad idea.

When Wally, my wife, and I got to the swingers' hotel, we stopped off at the registration desk and picked up a copy of the illustrated convention guide, which I personally would have killed for when I was in ninth grade. It listed the various seminars, including "Introduction to Tantra," "The Myth of Monogamy," "Meeting New Friends on the Internet," "The Benefits and Mechanics of Long-Term Polyamory," and "Basic Forklift Maintenance."

I am of course kidding about that last one, but I am not kidding when I say that this entire hotel had been taken over by swingers, hundreds of them. You could tell they were swingers because they were all wearing convention wristbands. In some cases, the wristband was the largest garment they were wearing. These were people of all ages and bodily types: Some had obviously spent a lot of time at the fitness club; whereas others appeared to have recently *eaten* a fitness club.

We had lunch at a table looking out on the pool area. Our conversation consisted almost entirely of us taking turns saying, "Ohmigod, look at THAT." We tried to be cool about it, but it is not easy to look cool when you're sticking a spoonful of soup in your ear because your head has just whirled sideways so your eyeballs could keep track of a passing thong.

The thong appears to be a major weapon in the swinger's fashion arsenal. This is not necessarily a good thing. Your taut-bodied individual may be able to pull it off (Har!), but when you see a portly middle-aged man who has more body hair than a musk ox AND (I swear) a tattoo of Elvis on his right butt cheek stroll past wearing essentially a No. 8 rubber band, you begin to think that maybe it's time Congress enacted strict Federal Thong Control.

Attire aside, most of the swingers seemed to be regular people. In fact, according to a story about the convention in the *Herald*, the two most-common professions for swingers are police officer and teacher. This stunned me, especially the teachers. I mean, remember when you were a kid, and you were shocked whenever you saw a teacher at say, the supermarket, because you didn't think of teachers as having any existence outside of school, or even necessarily as being food-eating life forms? Well, imagine if you encountered your trigonometry teacher wearing a garment that left absolutely nothing to the imagination regarding the cosine OR the hypotenuse.

I think that, as parents, we should be concerned about the fact this type of individual is being employed in our schools. Maybe we should notify the police.

No, wait.

Get the (Birthday) Party Started

TODAY'S PARENTING TOPIC IS: planning a birthday party for your two-year-old child.

The first thing you must decide, when planning a birthday party for a two-year-old is: Should you invite the two-year-old? Because a child that age can put a real damper on a party. And probably your child doesn't really understand that he or she is turning two. One of the best things about small children is that they have no clue how time works. My two-year-old daughter believes that everything that has ever happened, including her birth and the formation of the solar system, occurred "yesterday."

I have a friend named Helene who made excellent use of this phenomenon when her children were small. If they wanted to do something that, for whatever reason, they couldn't do, Helene, rather than argue, would tell them they could do it on "Tuesday." If her kids wanted to go swimming, and it was January, Helene would say: "We'll go swimming on Tuesday!" And they were satisfied, because they had a definite answer, even though it actually had no meaning. (Airport flight-information monitors are based on the same principle.)

Unfortunately, as people grow older, they come to understand the concept of time, unless they are my wife. (Just kidding!) (Not really!) But most two-year-olds have no idea what "two years old" means, and would not notice if you held their birthday party after they went to bed.

Another low-stress option is to wait until your child is invited to some OTHER two-year-old's birthday party, and when you get there, tell your child that the party is actually for him or her. ("Look, Jason! Your name is written right here on the cake! L-I-S-A!")

Of course the foregoing suggestions are intended in a purely humorous vein. (Not really!) Unless you are a Bad Parent, you must throw a birthday party for your two-year-old, and you must invite other two-year-olds, and THEY MUST HAVE FUN, even if they don't want to. This is why so many birthday parties feature rental clowns, even though few things are more terrifying to small children than a clown at close range. Stephen King based an entire novel on this concept.

Another fun thing that two-year-olds do not enjoy is organized activities. Most two-year-olds are happiest when they are free to wander around in a non-organized way. So it can be quite a chore to herd a group of them together for organized birthday fun. But you must do this, or the terrorists will have won.

When our daughter turned two, we had a big party at our house. That was over a month ago, and we're still finding cake frosting in unexpected places. ("So THAT'S why the VCR doesn't work!") Our house was filled with two-year-olds, running, falling, yelling, crying, pooping, etc., each with at least one adult in pursuit, trying to organize the child. I honestly didn't know who most of these children were, or how they found out about the party. Maybe the Internet. All I know is, the organized activity we had for them was: art. Yes! We invited small children to our house and DELIBERATELY GAVE THEM PAINT.

I believe the reason we did this is that our brains had been turned into coleslaw by the bouncy castle. A bouncy castle is a big rubber inflatable thing that you can rent for birthday parties, weddings, congressional hearings, etc. The idea is that children can climb inside and bounce around and have a lot of fun, unless they find the bouncy castle to be even more terrifying than the rental clown.

My daughter LOVED the bouncy castle. That was the good news. The bad news was, the rental company set it up at 8 A.M., six hours before the party started. Once my daughter realized there was a bouncy castle in her yard, she had to be inside it, bouncing, at all times, and she felt very strongly that there had to be a parent in there bouncing with her. So by the time the guests started arriving, my wife and I had spent about three hours apiece bouncing our IQs down into the low teens, which is why we thought it would be fun to give art supplies to two-year-olds. I'm surprised we didn't let them drive the car.

Of course, we also gave them cake, because this is mandatory at birthday parties, even though historically there is no known case of any two-year-old ever actually eating so much as a single molecule of

271

birthday cake. In fact, as far as I can tell, two-year-olds never eat *anything*. I think they nourish themselves via some kind of photosynthesis-like process that involves the direct absorption of Play-Doh.

In conclusion, holding a birthday party for two-year-olds is both fun and easy. All you have to do is follow a few simple steps! I will cover these on Tuesday.

It's Oscar Time —
Prepare the Blow Darts

Of all the prestigious awards that the entertainment industry gives to itself in humble recognition of its own sheer fabulousness — the Emmys, the Grammys, the Tonys, the Golden Globes, the Wallys, the Silver Spheres, the Vinnys, the Cubic Zirconium Orbs of Distinction, the Sneezys, and the Award That They Always Give to Kelsey Grammer — there is none so prestigious as the Oscars.

That's why an estimated 40 billion people will tune in this year to watch the Academy Awards show, which begins at 5 p.m. (Pacific) on March 24, with the climactic announcement of Best Picture scheduled to be announced at 8:30 P.M. (Pacific) on March 28.

Yes, it will be ninety-nine hours of nonstop entertainment, "Hollywood-style," broken down as follows:

- Movie stars reading spontaneous banter from TelePrompTers: 6 hours,

37 minutes.

- Shots of the always fascinating Jack Nicholson sitting in the audience: 4 hours, 19 minutes.
- Jokes involving Enron: 1 hour.
- Memorable, unscripted moments: 3 minutes.
- People you never heard of thanking other people you never heard of: 87 hours.
- Of course, this is the "best case" scenario; usually the show runs long. Nothing can be done about this. The producers have tried everything to pick up the pace, including, last year, sharpshooters. As soon as a winner's thank-you speech reached the two-minute mark, FWWWWT! A tranquilizer dart would lodge itself in his or her neck. But this did no good. The winner for Longest Short Foreign Film hung tough for more than 11 minutes, sustaining dart after dart until he looked like a tuxedo-wearing porcupine, but doggedly continuing to thank people, some apparently picked at random from a telephone directory, before staggering off the stage with enough sedative in his bloodstream to immobilize a water buffalo.

That's the kind of adrenaline rush you get at the Academy Awards. I know because I was there once, in 1987, along with the movie critics, who are very bitter because they know, in their hearts, that their teeth will never look as nice as the teeth of the people they write about. The critics are also angry because, in their opinion, the Oscars always go to the wrong people. Here's how they explained it to me: Each year, the Academy gives the awards to people who really should have won LAST year. The reason they didn't win last year was that the Academy was giving the awards to people who should have won the year before THAT. This has been going on all the way back to the first Academy Awards, which apparently were handed out by total morons.

Who deserves to win this year's awards? This is an especially difficult question this year, because there were so many fine performances and movies, and I have not seen any of them. My wife and I have a two-year-old daughter, and on those rare occasions when we have a babysitter, we use the time for activities we need to catch up on, such as brushing our teeth.

So the only movie I've seen this past year is *The Sound of Music*, from 1965, on DVD.

But I've seen it a LOT. It's my daughter's favorite movie. She thinks it's called "Boys and Girls," as in, "Watch Boys and Girls? Watch Boys and Girls? Watch Boys and Girls?" etc. We watch it eight or more times per day.

The Sound of Music is the heartwarming story, set in 1937, of the von Trapp family in Austria, where for some reason everybody speaks English with a British accent, except for the oldest von Trapp daughter, Liesl, who has a distinct American accent, possibly as a result of an accident that also caused her to lose a vowel. There is trouble in the von Trapp family because (a) the children don't know any songs, and (b) World War II is about to break out. Meanwhile Julie Andrews is studying to be a nun, but is having second thoughts because when she asks the head nun for advice, the head nun starts shrieking about climbing mountains in a voice that could bore holes through steel.

So Julie becomes the governess of the von Trapp children and wins them over by making clothes for them out of hideous draperies. Then she teaches them the song "Doe, a deer, a female deer" etc., which they sing, thanks to the DVD player's handy "repeat" button, over and over and over and over, until the Nazis flee, screaming, never to return. So it's a happy ending, and I hope we can say the same for this year's Academy Awards. Thanks for reading this. I also want to thank my agent, Al Hart, and FWWWWT . . .

Supersize Your Fries
with This Column?

The Surgeon General has released yet another report warning Americans that we're fat.

That's what your modern Surgeon General does: issue warnings. He sees danger lurking everywhere. Years ago, the Surgeon General was more laid-back; his staff often found him passed out under his desk at 2:30 in the afternoon, reeking of cigars and bourbon. He would go for years at a stretch without issuing a warning. Back then, Americans felt free to smoke, eat fatty foods, drink liquor, and drive cars without seat belts, often all at the same time. Granted, most of them died by age thirty-two. But they were carefree.

Today, of course, we have vigilant health authorities notifying us hourly that pretty much everything we do is fatal. And so we have the Surgeon General coming out with yet another official report — titled "Americans: What a Bunch of Whales" — which contains these shocking statistics:

- 61 percent of all adult Americans are overweight.
- One of these Americans always sits next to me on the airplane.
- This person uses 140 percent of the armrest.
- Americans don't really understand percentages, either.

What is causing these problems? For one thing, the Surgeon General notes, many schools no longer require students to take Physical Education. This is a crime. When I was a student, P.E. class was MANDATORY, with each class lasting 45 minutes, broken down as follows:

- Changing into gym uniforms: 16 minutes.
- Roll call, which always indicated perfect attendance because somebody shouted "Here!" in response to every name called, despite the fact that roughly 30 percent of the class was actually out behind the gym smoking cigarettes: 12 minutes.
- "Jumping Jacks": 2 minutes.
- Taking showers, snapping each other with towels, changing back to civilian clothes, causing lifetime psychic damage to some unfortunate student

by shoving him out into the hallway stark naked except for an athletic supporter on his head: 15 minutes.

Yes, it was a demanding physical regimen, and we followed it TWICE A WEEK. Little wonder that we brought the Soviet Union to its knees. So I totally agree with the Surgeon General about bringing back mandatory P.E. And not just for students. Cabinet members should also be included.

Where I do NOT agree with the Surgeon General is on his dietary recommendations. He's upset that Americans do not follow the Department of Agriculture's Food Guide Pyramid, which tells you in detail how many cups of whole grains, raw leafy vegetables, yogurt, etc. you're supposed to consume per day based on your age, weight, number of teeth, etc.

Let me respond, on behalf of all Americans, by suggesting, in the politest way possible, that the Surgeon General should go sit on the Food Guide Pyramid. Because out here in the real world, we do not carry cups around with us, nor do we encounter "whole grains," whatever THEY are. Here in the real world, we face dietary decisions such as: Do we want the Hungry Human Burger 'n' Bacon 'n' Cheese 'n'

Egg 'n' Sausage 'n' Slab o' Lard Combo Deluxe with a large order of fries? Or with a REALLY large order of fries?

Yes, real Americans need a more effective dietary aid than the Food Guide Pyramid. Here's my idea: We should use farmers. Lord knows we pay them enough. In the past five years, the Department of Agriculture paid 92 BILLION TAXPAYER-SUPPLIED DOLLARS in subsidies to farmers, including such hardscrabble sons of the soil as (I am not making this up) Scottie Pippen, who makes $18 million a year playing basketball, and who got $131,575 in farm subsidies; and Ted Turner, who is worth more than $6 billion, and who got $176,077 in subsidies.

So here's my proposal: Any farmer who (a) receives taxpayer money and (b) is worth more than $1 million should be required to spend ten hours per week actively preventing taxpayers from eating so much. Picture the scene: You're in the convenience store. You grab a package of Hostess brand Ding Dongs. You're heading for the checkout counter, and . . . BAM, you're grabbed from behind by Ted Turner! So you turn around and whomp him on the head with a 16-ounce jar of Kraft brand jalapeño-flavored Cheez Whiz.

As he goes down like a sack of whole grain, you grab a bottle of Yoo-hoo brand Yoo-hoo, pay the cashier, and lumber out of the store.

That's how I'd handle this national weight problem. I have plenty of other ideas for improving our health, so if the Surgeon General is reading this: Sir, please feel free to get in touch. You can reach me under my desk.

North Dakota Wants Its
Place in the Sun

North Dakota is talking about changing its name. I frankly didn't know you could do that. I thought states' names were decreed by the Bible or something. In fact, as a child I believed that when Columbus arrived in North America, the states' names were actually, physically, written on the continent, in gigantic letters, the way they are on maps. I still think this would be a good idea, because if an airplane's navigational system failed, the pilot could just look out the window and see exactly where the plane was. ("Okay, there's a huge 'W' down there, so we're over Wyoming. Or Wisconsin.")

But apparently states can change their names, and some North Dakotans want to change "North Dakota." Specifically, they don't like the word "North," which connotes a certain northness. In the words of North Dakota's former governor, Ed Schafer: "People have such an instant thing about how North Dakota is cold and snowy and flat."

We should heed the words of the former governor, and not just because the letters in "Ed Schafer" can be rearranged to spell "Shed Farce." The truth is that when we think about North Dakota, which is not often, we picture it as having the same year-round climate as Uranus.

In contrast, SOUTH Dakota is universally believed to be a tropical paradise with palm trees swaying on surf-kissed beaches. Millions of tourists, lured by the word "South," flock to South Dakota every winter, often wearing nothing but skimpy bathing suits. Within hours, most of them die and become covered with snow, not to be found until spring, when they cause a major headache for South Dakota's farmers by clogging up the cultivating machines. South Dakota put a giant fence around the whole state to keep these tourists out, and STILL they keep coming. That's how powerful a name can be.

I'll give you another example. I live in Florida, where we have BIG cockroaches.

Q. How big are they?

A. They are so big that, when they back up, they are required by federal law to emit warning beeps.

These cockroaches could harm Florida's

image. But we Floridians solved that problem by giving them a new name, "palmetto bugs," which makes them sound cute and harmless. So when a guest walks into a Florida kitchen and screams at the sight of an insect the size of Charles Barkley, we say: "Don't worry! It's just a palmetto bug!" And then we and our guest have a hearty laugh, because we know there's nothing to worry about, as long as we do not make any sudden moves toward the palmetto bug's sandwich.

So changing names is a sound idea, an idea based on the scientific principle that underlies the field of marketing, which is: People are stupid. Marketing experts know that if you call something by a different name, *people will believe it's a different thing.* That's how "undertakers" became "funeral directors." That's how "trailers" became "manufactured housing." That's how "We're putting you on hold for the next decade" became "Your call is important to us."

And that's why some North Dakotans want to give the state a new name, a name that will give the state a more positive, inviting, and forward-looking image. That name is: "Palmetto Bug."

No, seriously, they want to drop the

"North" and call the state, simply, "Dakota." I think this change is brilliant, and could also work for other states with image problems. New Jersey, for example, should call itself, simply, "New."

Be advised that "Dakota" is not the first shrewd marketing concept thought up by North Dakotans. Are you familiar with Grand Forks, North Dakota? No? It's located just west of East Grand Forks, Minnesota. According to a letter I received from a Grand Forks resident who asked to remain nameless ("I have to live here," he wrote), these cities decided they needed to improve their image, and the result was — get ready — "The Grand Cities."

The Grand Cities, needless to say, have a website **(grandcities.net),** where you can read sentences about The Grand Cities written in MarketingSpeak, which is sort of like English, except that it doesn't actually mean anything. Here's an actual quote: "It's the intersection of earth and sky. It's a glimpse of what lies ahead. It's hope, anticipation, and curiosity reaching out to you in mysterious ways. Timeless. Endless. Always enriching your soul. Here, where the earth meets the sky, the Grand Cities of Grand Forks, North Dakota, and East Grand Forks, Minnesota."

Doesn't that just make you want to cancel that trip to Paris or Rome and head for The Grand Cities? As a resident of Florida ("Where the earth meets the water and forms mud") I am definitely planning to go to Dakota. I want to know what they're smoking up there.

There's a Hoover Dam . . . and Now, the Dave Sewage Lifter

North Dakota is calling me. "Come on up!" it says. And then it adds: "Bring thermal underwear!"

This invitation resulted from a column in which I poked fun at North Dakota for wanting to drop the word "North" from its name, so that people will stop thinking of it as a cold, frigid, freezing, subzero, arctic, polar, wintry place characterized by low temperatures. My column also made fun of Grand Forks, North Dakota, and East Grand Forks, Minnesota, for marketing themselves as "The Grand Cities" and proclaiming that they are "where the earth meets the sky." My feeling was that there are a LOT of places where the earth meets the sky, including most municipal landfills, but you don't see them bragging about it.

Anyway, that column got a BIG response. I got mail from every resident of

North Dakota (a total of almost 150 letters). Many of these letters proudly defended North Dakota and its citizens (sample quote: "The people are friendly and warm-hearted. We don't usually shoot tourists like some other states").

Several Grand Cities political and civic leaders invited me to visit. They sent me information about the area, as well as gifts of typical North Dakota things, including a plastic baggie filled with peat. Peat is a substance that looks like frog poop but is actually formed from decayed swamp plants and is used as a fuel. Either that, or the North Dakotans, as a prank, sent me a baggie full of frog poop, hoping that I would set fire to it.

Another traditional North Dakota item I received was buffalo jerky, which is a delicacy made from the jerky of a buffalo. If you are ever, at gunpoint, forced to choose between eating buffalo jerky and eating peat, my advice is: Go with the peat.

The jerky was sent by the mayor of Grand Forks, Mike Brown, who also made this generous offer: If I visit his city, he will name a sewage lift station after me. Really. According to the mayor, this is a major honor in Grand Forks. "That system moves eight million gallons of sewage a day," he said, in a statement that tells us more than perhaps we want to know about the effects of jerky consumption on the human digestive system.

But having my name on a sewage lifter is not the only reason why I am attracted to the Grand Cities. There are a LOT of exciting things going on up there. It's like Paris, Disney World, and Las Vegas all rolled into one, minus the hotels, restaurants, attractions, Louvre museum, roads, etc.

But who needs attractions, when you have . . . Cats Incredible! This is a HUGE annual summer event in the Grand Cities, judging from the *Grand Forks Herald*, which covers Cats Incredible in front-page stories with headlines the height of Bette Midler. As well it should. Because Cats Incredible is nothing less than the largest catfish tournament in the entire Grand Cities region, attracting thousands of spectators. When that many people turn out to watch other people fish, then you know you're talking about an area with poor TV reception.

No, seriously, Cats Incredible looks very exciting. The *Herald* ran a front-page photo of this year's winning team — two men holding a fish that is WAY uglier than the thing that's always chasing Sigourney Weaver around the spaceship. The *Herald* article describes one of the winning anglers as "a catfish guide, seminar speaker, and author."

Yes! Catfish seminars! Don't tell ME this is not a great country.

If you think Cats Incredible is the only excitement going on up there, think again. Because the Grand Cities also play host to — this is a real event — the Frosty Bobber. In a stark departure from the concept of Cats Incredible, which is a summer fishing tournament, the Frosty Bobber is . . . a winter fishing tournament! It gets its name from the fact that, if you spend enough time sitting next to a hole in the ice, eventually your bobber gets frosty. This is why there are so few Canadians.

And there is much, much more to the Grand Cities. There is also the annual Potato Bowl, which I am sure is everything the name implies. And the mayor of East Grand Forks, Minnesota, Lynn Stauss, informs me that his city also boasts some powerful attractants, including "the largest beet sugar processing plant in the United States."

So call me crazy, but I'm seriously pondering a trip up to Dakota. I could use

some excitement, not to mention some
fresh air. Because this peat smoke is disgusting.

N.D.'s New Barry Building
Takes Your Breath Away

My advice to aspiring humor columnists is: Never make fun of North Dakota. Because the North Dakotans will invite you, nicely but relentlessly, to visit, and eventually you'll have to accept. When you get there, they'll be incredibly nice to you, treating you with such warmth and hospitality that before long you feel almost like family. Then they will try to asphyxiate you with sewer gas.

I found this out when I went to Grand Forks, North Dakota, in January. I had made fun of Grand Forks and its sister city, East Grand Forks, Minnesota, for calling themselves the Grand Cities and declaring that they are "where the earth meets the sky." (This turns out to be slightly inaccurate: In between the earth and the sky, there's a layer of really hard ice.)

I arrived at Grand Forks International Airport on a subzero Tuesday night. I have never been so cold in my life. And that was *inside the terminal.* Outside it was much worse. I'm pretty sure wolves were stalking me as I staggered across the wind-whipped parking lot, wondering if there could be a colder place on the planet. Unfortunately, there was: the interior of my rental car, which had liquid oxygen on the seats.

The way the North Dakotans deal with this is to leave their cars running. The state fuel-economy average must be around .000003 miles per gallon, because everywhere you go, you see unattended cars with the motors running. Many people start their cars with remote-control devices, but I believe that some of the smarter cars also spontaneously start themselves to keep warm.

The thing is, nobody steals the unattended cars, or anything else. During my visit, roughly once every four minutes a North Dakotan would remind me, in a nice way, that they have hardly any crime up there, in stark contrast to my city, Miami, where, as the North Dakotans understand it, you can't hear yourself think for all the machine-gun fire. But I can't argue with them: It does feel very safe up there, and everybody does seem to get along, despite the fact that the population is quite diverse, ranging all the way from people whose ancestors immigrated from Norway, to people whose ancestors immigrated from a different part of Norway.

I spent part of a day driving around the Greater Grand Forks area, where you can see many breathtakingly spectacular vistas if you have taken hallucinogenic drugs. Otherwise you'll see a lot of really flat agriculture covered by snow. But the people, as I may have mentioned, are very nice, and I saw absolutely no crimes committed, even though there were many cultivating machines sitting around unattended.

The Grand Cities themselves are more urban, featuring stores, restaurants, and other buildings, with the occasional unattended car running outside. The Grand Cities are trying hard to attract more tourists and businesses, so I urge everybody to go up there and check it out. There is PLENTY of parking.

Without question the most memorable experience I had in Grand Forks was a public ceremony in which a municipal sewage pumping station was formally named after me. I am not making this up. They took me in a limousine to the station, where more than one hundred people had gathered, despite the fact that the temperature was an estimated 8,500 degrees below zero.

The mayor of Grand Forks, Mike Brown, who is also an obstetrician/gynecologist, read a nice speech in which he flatteringly compared my work to the production of excrement. Then came the big moment when I unveiled a big sign on the side of the building, with large letters stating: DAVE BARRY LIFT STATION NO. 16.

Words cannot convey what it feels like to look at a building with your name on it — a building capable of pumping 450,000 gallons of untreated sewage per *day* — and at the same time hear the unmistakable WHUPWHUPWHUP of North Dakotans enthusiastically applauding with heavy gloves. It was a wonderful occasion, until they took me on an official tour of the pumping station. When they opened the door, WHOOSH, we were engulfed by a cloud of pent-up fumes from the Outhouse from Hell. Trees wilted as far away as Wisconsin.

Fortunately I survived, and went on to have several more memorable experiences in the Grand Cities. Next week I'll tell you about the sport of ice fishing, which is irrefutable proof that prolonged exposure to cold causes brain damage. I'll also describe a tradition called the "potluck supper," which poses a serious threat to the world's dwindling reserves of Jell-O. Until then, keep your engines running.

Steve's Schnapps Kept the Frost Off Dave's Bobber

In last week's column, I described my January visit to Grand Forks, North Dakota, and East Grand Forks, Minnesota, which are also called "The Grand Cities" by about six people who are hoping this name will attract more humans to the area.

I went to the Grand Cities because I had poked some good-natured fun at the residents. They responded by good-naturedly inviting me up and formally naming a sewage pumping station after me in a ceremony that will forever remain a vivid memory in my mind, even though I have burned my clothes.

But that was not the end of their hospitality. They also exposed me to the popular northern sport of ice fishing, which gets its name from the fact that "ice fishing" sounds better than "sitting around drinking."

The idea behind ice fishing is that the northern winter, which typically lasts forty-three months, eventually starts to make a guy feel cooped up inside his house. So he goes out to the Great Outdoors, drills a hole in a frozen body of water, drops in a line, and then coops himself up inside a tiny structure called a "fish house" with a heater and some fishing buddies and some cigars and some adult beverages and maybe a TV with a satellite dish. It's basically the same thing as drilling a hole in the floor of your recreation room, the difference being that in your recreation room you'd have a better chance of catching a fish.

I started my ice-fishing trip at the Cabela's outdoor-supply store, which is close to the biggest thing in East Grand Forks, and which has huge tanks inside with fish swimming around. There I met a guy named Steve Gander, who had two snowmobiles running outside in the subzero cold. We hopped on and drove them at a high rate of speed, right through the East Grand Forks traffic. (By "the East Grand Forks traffic," I mean, "a car.")

We snowmobiled down to the Red River, which divides East Grand Forks from Grand Forks, and which gets its name from the fact that the water is brown. There we met Cabela's employee Matt Gindorff, who had drilled some holes in the ice. Matt dropped a fishing line into a hole, and within just fifteen minutes — talk about beginner's luck! — nothing happened. Nothing ever happens in ice fishing, because — this is my theory — there are no fish under the ice. Fish are not rocket scientists, but they are smart enough to spend the winter someplace warm, like Arizona. The only fish anywhere near me and Matt were the ones in the tanks at Cabela's; they were probably looking out the window at us, thinking, "What a pair of MORONS."

TRUE FACT: Every January, The Grand Cities hold a day-long ice-fishing tournament called "The Frosty Bobber." The first year it was held, the total number of fish caught was zero. The second year, one person actually did catch something. It was a salamander.

So Matt and I sat there, "fishing," until our body temperatures had dropped to about 55 degrees. Fortunately, Steve had brought along a traditional beverage called "schnapps," which can be used, in a pinch, to fuel your snowmobile.

After the "fishing," Steve and I

snowmobiled up to the Sacred Heart School, where the Grand Cities honored me with a benefit potluck supper, to which the entire community had been invited. It was a big deal. The *Grand Forks Herald* published a color-coded map that divided the Grand Cities into three sectors, and assigned the residents of each sector to bring one of the three basic potluck food groups: (1) Hotdish; (2) Jell-O salad; and (3) Bars, which are desserts cut into bars, and which often feature, as a key culinary ingredient, Rice Krispies.

The potluck supper was almost a disaster, because the people who showed up first were all from the east side, which had been assigned to bring bars. This meant that for a while there, there were hardly any hot dishes. This story was reported the next day on the front page of the *Grand Forks Herald*, under the headline (I am not making any of this up) "HOT-DISH SCARE."

Fortunately, the hot dish people showed up. So did the Jell-O people, big time. I have never seen that much Jell-O in my life. Most of it had things suspended in it: fruits, vegetables, office supplies, you name it. But the food was delicious, and the people were wonderful to me. As I sat there in the Sacred Heart gym, surrounded by these good-hearted, hard-working, Jell-O-eating people, I felt, despite my big-city cynicism, a warm glow inside. You have GOT to try schnapps.

Send in Your Weasel Jokes (Unless You're Canadian)

The scientific community, having run out of things to clone, is now trying to identify the World's Funniest Joke. I refer to a project called Laugh Lab, being conducted by Dr. Richard Wiseman of the University of Hertfordshire (pronounced "Scotland").

Dr. Wiseman has set up an Internet site, **www.laughlab.co.uk/home.html,** that has received more than 10,000 jokes, which have been rated by more than 100,000 people, most of them wrong. I say this because the joke they have so far rated as the funniest is this:

"Sherlock Holmes and Dr. Watson are going camping. They pitch their tent under the stars and go to sleep. Sometime in the middle of the night Holmes wakes Watson up. 'Watson, look up at the stars, and tell me what you deduce.' Watson says, 'I see millions of stars and even if a few of those have planets, it's quite likely there are some planets like Earth, and if there are a few planets like Earth out there, there might also be life.' Holmes replied: 'Watson, you idiot, somebody stole our tent!' "

Now, I'm not saying this is a bad joke. I'm just saying this is not even close to being the funniest joke in the world. It would be funnier if Holmes woke Watson up and said, "Watson, there's a weasel chomping on my privates!" I'm not sure where the joke would go from there, but you can't go wrong with a setup like that.

Of course, some would disagree. And when I say "some," I of course mean "women." Women generally dislike groin-ular humor; this is one of the startling findings — and when I say "startling" I mean "not startling" — of the Laugh Lab project. I have been listening to people — and when I say "people," I mean "men" — tell jokes for longer than fifty years (I don't mean the jokes take longer than fifty years to tell, although some of them come close) and I can state for a scientific fact that the funnier a joke is, the more likely a woman is to react by saying: "That's disgusting!" As if that's a BAD thing.

According to a Laugh Lab press release, women don't like jokes that involve aggression, sexuality, or offensiveness — also known as "the three building blocks of humor." The release states that women prefer "jokes involving word plays." It gives the following example of a joke that women like, but men dislike:

"A man had a dog called Minton. One day Minton ate two shuttlecocks. When the owner found out he said 'Bad Minton!!' "

Whoo-HOO! "Bad Minton!!" Get it? Here, sniff these smelling salts.

I'll tell you who else has a serious humor deficiency: Canada. I say this because, according to Laugh Lab, the following joke was rated highest by Canadians: "What do you call a woman who can balance four pints of beer on her head? Beatrix."

Get it? "Beatrix!" Which sounds sort of, but not quite enough, like "Beer Tricks!" Ha ha! Maybe it would be funnier if they called her "Minton."

Laugh Lab also had people rate jokes that were generated by a computer. This is important research, because if computers can produce workable jokes, humanity may finally see the long-awaited day when humor columnists have to work even less than they do now. Unfortunately, the highest-rated joke that the computer produced was: "What kind of murderer has fiber? A cereal killer."

Granted, that's better than what Canada came up with. But it's not up to the standards of, say, Yemen.

Anyway, if you want to participate in the Laugh Lab project, you can go to the Internet site and rate some jokes. But I warn you: Don't have food in your mouth! Because the hilarity level of these jokes is sure to make you go: "Huh!" For example, here's one I was asked to rate: "Why do elephants have big ears? Noddy wouldn't pay the ransom." Allegedly this joke is funny in England, which uses metric humor.

But here's the good part: You can also SUBMIT a joke to the Laugh Lab. In the interest of improving the overall joke quality, I urge everybody reading this column to submit a joke incorporating some variation of the phrase: "There's a weasel chomping on my privates." (Example: "Why do elephants have big ears? Because there's a weasel chomping on their privates.") Also, if you see this phrase in a joke you're being asked to rate, give that joke the highest rating. Do it now. Do it for humanity. Do it for the most noble of all possible reasons: To get to the other side.

Penelope Cruz Is NOT Having Dave's Baby

Before all these rumors and innuendoes get out of hand, I want to set the record straight regarding me and Penelope Cruz.

In case you have not heard, Penelope and I recently were both on the *Today* show on exactly the same day. As I am sure you are aware, Penelope is a top female star who has been romantically linked to Tom Cruise. Prior to that, she was romantically linked to Matt Damon and Nicolas Cage. Penelope is just one of those female celebrities who are natural linkers. Whenever she gets into a confined space with a male celebrity, boom, they become linked, and nothing can separate them, until another male celebrity comes within range.

So as you can imagine, the *Today* show created a potentially torrid situation when it booked both me and Penelope to appear on the show only minutes apart. She was there to promote her latest movie by being glamorous and charming; I was there to promote my latest book by making flatulence noises with my hands. You could have cut the sexual tension with a meat cleaver.

But let me make this very clear: Penelope and I did not experience any kind of linkage. For one thing, we are both very happy in our current relationships. For another thing, we did not, technically, meet. Yes, there was a brief, tension-charged moment when I glimpsed a dark object that I have reason to believe was the back of Penelope's head. I can't say for sure, because Penelope was surrounded by an entourage the size of my high-school graduating class. But that is all that happened. So I am calling upon the international news media to stop spreading these vicious rumors, which can only cause pain to me, and Penelope, and Tom, and their respective entourages. We have all suffered enough.

Now that I've cleared that up, you probably want to hear about the other celebrities I met that morning, and what they were like in person. Probably the biggest name was the late George Harrison of the Beatles, whose sister, Louise, was on the show. I rode in the elevator with her, in person, and although we did not speak, she seemed very nice.

Also on the show was Julia Roberts, but she had been videotaped earlier, so I can't tell you what she was like in person. I can tell you that, on the videotape, which I watched in person, she seemed to be not at all "stuck-up," and very easy for Katie Couric to talk to. In person, Katie Couric — and you may quote me on this — is very nice.

I personally shook hands with Al Roker, the jovial and portly NBC weatherman. I would imagine that, at one time or another in his career, Al has shaken hands with many top celebrities, including Brad Pitt, the Backstreet Boys, Britney Spears, Donald Rumsfeld, and "J. Lo," although none of them were there on this particular morning. Nevertheless, in person, Al was every bit as jovial and portly as you would hope.

One little celebrity "tidbit" that I can pass along — and I know this is true, because she looked me right in the eye and told me so herself — is that Claudia Kaneb, the wardrobe person at the *Today* show, who personally removed the dandruff flakes from my sport jacket, has also, in her career, worked on sport jackets belonging to Mr. Geraldo Rivera. I asked

Claudia what they were like, in person, and she told me that they were — and this is a direct quote — "very nice jackets."

I was interviewed by Bob Costas, who was filling in for Matt Lauer, who was on vacation at an undisclosed location, which I am sure is very nice. While we were off-camera, Bob brought up a column I wrote about baseball several months ago in which I mentioned Bob's name in connection with the song "Who Let the Dogs Out?" by the Baha Men. Bob stressed to me that he has nothing to do with that song. So let me state for the record: BOB COSTAS IS NOT NOW, NOR HAS HE EVER BEEN, ONE OF THE BAHA MEN. Although I am sure they are nice.

After I got off the air, I called my wife to ask her how I did on national television. My wife did not want to talk about that. All she wanted to talk about was whether I thought Penelope Cruz is as beautiful as everybody else seems to think she is. I assured her that, from what I could tell, Penelope, in person, is a woofing dog. I try to be nice, but I am not a total idiot.

Learning to Love the Computer, Warts and All

At least once per day, without fail, my computer, like every computer I have ever owned, has some kind of emotional breakdown. It simply stops working — often when I'm not touching it — and it puts a message on the screen informing me that an error has occurred. It does not say what the error is, nor where it occurred. For all I know, it occurred in New Zealand, and my computer found out about it via the Internet, and became so upset that it could not go on.

When this happens, I have to turn my computer off and start it up again. When I do, my computer puts a snippy note on the screen informing me that it is scanning its disks for errors, because it was shut down improperly.

"But I DIDN'T DO ANYTHING!" I shout, but my computer ignores me, because it is busy scanning its disks. You just know that if it finds any errors, it's going to blame me, even though I don't even know where its disks ARE.

While my computer is busy, I scan my wart. I have a wart on my right leg. It has been there for many years. I call it Buddy. I keep an eye on Buddy, in case his appearance changes. I've read that it's a bad thing, medically, when a wart suddenly changes appearance. If I ever look down and see that Buddy has turned green, or he's wearing a little pair of Groucho glasses, I'll know it's time to take some kind of medical action. Such as quit drinking.

But my point is that because of computer weirdness, I regularly see an entire morning's work — sometimes as many as eighteen words — get blipped away forever to the Planet of Lost Data. Needless to say, I use Microsoft Windows. I've been a loyal Windows man since the first version, which required you to write on the screen with crayons. Every year or so, Microsoft comes out with a new version, which Microsoft always swears is better and more reliable, and I always buy it. I bought Windows 2.0, Windows 3.0, Windows 3.1415926, Windows 95, Windows 98, Windows ME, Windows RSVP, The Best of Windows, Windows Strikes Back, Windows Does Dallas, and Windows Let's All Buy Bill Gates a House the Size of Vermont.

My computers keep having seizures, but I keep buying Windows versions, hoping I'll get lucky. I'm like the loser in the nightclub who keeps hitting on the hot babe. His shoes are squishing from the piña colada she poured on him, but he's thinking: "She's warming up to me!"

I bring this all up because now Microsoft has a new version out, Windows XP, which according to everybody is the "most reliable Windows ever." To me, this is like saying that asparagus is "the most articulate vegetable ever." But still, I am tempted. "Maybe this will be the one," I say to Buddy, as the two of us wait for the disks to be scanned.

If I do get Windows XP, I won't try to install it myself. I no longer mess with the innards of my computer. The last time I tried was a disaster, even though I enlisted the aid of my friend Rob Stavis, a medical doctor who is the most mechanically inclined person I know. Rob can disassemble and successfully reassemble a live human being. He and I recently spent an entire weekend trying to solve an allegedly simple computer problem. We wound up at the computer store, talking to guys who were trained by the Monty Python Institute of Customer Service:

US: So, what do we need to make it work?

THEM: You need a model FRT–2038 expostulating refrembulator.

US: And that will make it work?

THEM: No.

Finally, I hired a guy named J.C., who is a Microsoft Certified Technician. He was in my office for the better part of two days, most of it on the phone with Technical Support. It was fascinating for me, a layperson, to hear the technical terminology that J.C. used to get the information he needed: "DO NOT PUT ME ON HOLD, DO YOU HEAR ME? DO NOT PUT ME ON HO . . . HELLO? HELLO?? YOU (very nontechnical term)!"

In the end, J.C. solved the problem. So now I'm thinking about hiring him again. Because the more I think about this Windows XP, the better it looks, sitting over there by the bar, drinking a piña colada. All I have to do is make my move, and I'll have what every guy dreams of: computer reliability!

I worry about who will take care of Buddy.

It's All About Cloning, Not Clowning

Human cloning: Will it be a lifesaving scientific advance, like penicillin? Or will it prove to be a horrible mistake that unleashes untold devastation upon humanity, like the accordion?

As American citizens, we need to form strong opinions about this issue, so that we can write letters to our congresspersons, so that their staffs can, as a precautionary measure, burn them. But first we must inform ourselves by asking questions and then answering them in the "Q" and "A" format.

Q. Does Tom Cruise shave his chest?

A. We meant questions about cloning.

Q. Oh, okay. What is cloning?

A. In scientific terms, it is a procedure by which a theoretically infinite number of genetically identical organisms emerge, one at a time, from a Volkswagen Beetle.

Q. No, that's "clowning."

A. Whoops! Our bad! Cloning is a procedure whereby scientists, using tweezers, manipulate DNA, which is a tiny genetic code that is found in all living things as well as crime scenes that have been visted by O. J. Simpson. A single strand of DNA can be used to create a whole new organism, as was proved when scientists at Stanford University took DNA from the fingernail of a deceased man and grew a six-foot-tall, 190-pound fingernail. Unfortunately, it escaped from the laboratory and held police at bay for hours by screeching itself against a blackboard. It was finally subdued by National Guard troops equipped with ear plugs and a huge emery board.

Q. Have scientists cloned any other organisms?

A. In 1997, a group of Scottish scientists cloned a sheep named Dolly, which was genetically identical to the original sheep.

Q. How could they tell?

A. They had the original farmer take a hard look at it, and he said, quote: "That's her, all right!"

Q. Wow.

A. Of course, he said the same thing

about one of the scientists.

Q. Have there been any other successful cloning experiments?

A. Yes. In 1995, scientists in Florida used a single strand of DNA from the Backstreet Boys to form 'N Sync. Or maybe it was the other way around.

Q. What about humans?

A. We are getting very close. Recently, a firm in Massachusetts announced that it had cloned some human embryos. However, these embryos were alive for only a few hours, and stopped growing after they had formed microscopic six-cell spheres.

Q. What did the firm do with them?

A. They are currently working in Customer Service.

Q. Is anybody else trying to clone humans?

A. Yes. A group called the "Raelians," which was founded in France, and which we are not making up, claims to be working on a human-cloning project. According to their Internet site **(www.rael.org),** the Raelians are named for a French journalist named Rael who, in 1973, "was contacted by a visitor from another planet." This visitor informed Rael that human life was brought to Earth by aliens, who will come back and visit us if we build them an embassy. The Raelians estimate that this will cost $20 million, and would appreciate donations for this vital mission.

Q. Where does the U.S. government stand on this issue?

A. There is growing bipartisan support for a nuclear strike against France.

Q. Speaking of wacko cults, do you think Tom Cruise is so handsome?

A. We think he is a little chest-shaving weasel, but when we ask our spouse to confirm this, she just gets this dreamy look in her eyes.

Q. How do you, personally, feel about human cloning?

A. Why do you think we refer to ourselves in the plural?

Book-Tour Blues:
My Kingdom for a
100-Watt Lightbulb

I recently spent several weeks on a book tour, flying around the country with a suitcase full of increasingly alarming underwear. I'm pleased to report that airport security remains highly effective, especially as regards the terrorist threat posed by eighty-seven-year-old women with the mobility of oak trees. Because these women need extra time to reach their seats, they are — as instructed by the pre-boarding announcement — first in line to board the plane, and thus they almost always get picked for "random" screening by the security personnel, who need to reach their quota so they can get back to standing around.

We frequent fliers have figured this system out, and we lag behind the elderly women, who dodder forward cluelessly, cannon fodder in the War on Terror. They are pulled aside and stand, bewildered, as security personnel wand them and root through their denture adhesive while we able-bodied males stroll onto the plane. Granted, this system is insane, but we must not let sanity stand in the way of airport security.

Speaking of insane: One of my stops on the book tour was New York City, where the publisher put me at an extremely hip hotel. It's so hip that there is no sign outside saying HOTEL. I walked right past it the first time. Evidently if you're hip, you just know there's a hotel there.

The lobby was full of hip people on stark, modernistic furniture, talking into cellphones. They were all twenty-five years old, and they all wore black. I suspect their underwear is black. I myself was wearing khaki pants. I felt like a pig farmer in town for the big manure-spreader show.

The worst part was that I couldn't see. At some point in recent years, light must have become unhip, because this was the darkest hotel I've ever stayed in. The lobby wasn't so bad, but the elevator was so dimly lit that I had to put on my reading glasses, squat, and put my face right next to the buttons to find the one for my floor. I'm sure this amused the hip lobby people.

("Look! A pig farmer squatting in the elevator!")

My floor was actually scary. Have you ever been in one of those Halloween fun houses, where it's pitch-black and people leap out of the darkness to frighten you? The hotel hallway was like that. It was so dark that I honestly could not see my feet. I initially thought the walls were painted black, although I was later informed that they were very dark purple (a hip color). Sometimes I would encounter other guests in the hallway, but of course I could not see them because they were wearing black. I knew they were there only because I could hear their cellphones ringing.

My room had stark, modernistic furniture and several modernistic, low-wattage lamps, which, when I turned them all on, provided about the same illumination as a radio dial. The only way to read was to turn the TV on and tune it to a program with bright colors, such as *Baywatch*. My room was strewn with hip items, many of them for sale, including a hotel T-shirt (black), various herbal substances, and an "Intimacy Kit" for $12. If they really want to make money, they should sell 100-watt light bulbs; I would have paid $20 for one. They did sell a candle, labeled "TRAVEL

CANDLE," for $15; I considered buying it and using it in the elevator, to find the "Lobby" button.

My situation improved in California, where I stayed at a swank Beverly Hills hotel that had lights. It also had a swank bar jammed to the walls with fortyish movie executives who all wore (there must have been a memo) black pants, black shirts, and black leather jackets. They were talking about film projects with young, gifted blond women wearing attire that conveyed the message: "Take a look at THESE gifts!" Everybody was drinking — really — watermelon martinis. So I was still out of place ("Look! A pig farmer drinking beer!"). But at least I could see.

IRRELEVANT FINAL BOOK-TOUR NOTE: You know how, at drugstore cash registers, there are little displays of breath mints, batteries, etc., to encourage impulse buys? Well, in Los Angeles, I went into a Longs drugstore where the product on display at the cash register was: a sofa. Really. Suspended ominously right behind the cashier's head was a full-size sofa, priced at $499. Apparently this is for the harried shopper who gets to the cashier and goes, "Let's see . . . dental floss, aspirin, and . . . Ohmigosh! I almost forgot the sofa!" I should write a clever final sentence here, but I need to do my laundry.

We come, finally, to two essays I wrote about September 11, 2001. I wrote the first on the day after the attacks, in a state of shock and anger, not to mention serious doubt about whether there was anything meaningful that *anybody* — let alone a humor columnist — could say about this horrible thing.

I wrote the second essay almost a year later, when the *Herald* asked me to write something for the one-year anniversary. I realize this is a pretty somber way to end a humor book, but it didn't seem right to follow these essays with more jokes.

Just for Being
Americans . . .

No humor column today. I don't want to write it, and you don't want to read it.

No words of wisdom, either. I wish I were wise enough to say something that would help make sense of this horror, something that would help ease the unimaginable pain of the victims' loved ones, but I'm not that wise. I'm barely capable of thinking. Like many others, I've spent the hours since Tuesday morning staring at the television screen, sometimes crying, sometimes furious, but mostly just stunned.

What I can't get out of my mind is the fact that they used *our own planes*. I grew up in the Cold War, when we always pictured the threat as coming in the form of missiles — sleek, efficient death machines, unmanned, hurtling over the North Pole from far away. But what came, instead, were our own commercial airliners, big friendly flying buses coming from Newark and Boston with innocent people on board. Red, white, and blue planes, with "United" and "American" written on the side. The planes you've flown in and I've flown in. That's what they used to attack us. They were able to do it in part because our airport security is pathetic. But mainly they were able to do it because we are an open and trusting society that simply is not set up to cope with evil men, right here among us, who want to kill as many Americans as they can.

That's what's so hard to comprehend: *They want us to die just for being Americans.* They don't care which Americans die: military Americans, civilian Americans, young Americans, old Americans, baby Americans. They don't care. To them, we're all mortal enemies. The truth is that most Americans, until Tuesday, were only dimly aware of their existence, and posed no threat to them. But that doesn't matter to them; all that matters is that we're Americans. And so they used our own planes to kill us.

And then their supporters celebrated in the streets.

I'm not naïve about my country. My country is definitely not always right; my country has at times been terribly wrong.

But I know this about Americans: We don't set out to kill innocent people. We don't cheer when innocent people die.

The people who did this to us are monsters; the people who cheered them have hate-sickened minds. One reason they can cheer is that they know we would never do to them what their heroes did to us, even though we could, a thousand times worse. They know that when we hunt down the monsters, we will try hard not to harm the innocent. Those are the handcuffs we willingly wear, because for all our flaws, we are a decent people.

And now we are a traumatized people. The TV commentators keep saying that the attacks have awakened a "sleeping giant." And I guess we do look like a giant, to the rest of the world. But when I look around, I don't see a giant: I see millions of individuals — the resilient and caring citizens of New York and Washington; the incredibly brave firefighters, police officers, and rescue workers risking their lives in the dust and flames; the politicians standing on the steps of the Capitol and singing an off-key rendition of "God Bless America" that, corny as it was, had me weeping; the reporters and photographers who have not slept, and will not sleep, as long as there is

news to report; the people in my community, and communities across America,
lining up to give blood, wishing they could
do more.

No, I don't see a giant. What I see is
Americans. We may have the power of a
giant, but we also have the heart of a good
and generous people, and we will get
through this. We will grieve for our dead,
and tend to our wounded, and repair the
damage, and tighten our security, and put
our planes back in the air. Eventually most
of us, the ones lucky enough not to have
lost somebody, will resume our lives. Some
day, our country will track down the rest of
the monsters behind this, and make them
pay, and I suppose that will make most of
us feel a little better. But revenge and
hatred won't be why we'll go on. We'll go
on because we know this is a good country,
a country worth keeping.

Those who would destroy it only make
us see more clearly how precious it is.

Hallowed Ground

On a humid July day in Pennsylvania, hundreds of tourists, as millions have before them, are drifting among the simple gravestones and timeworn monuments of the national cemetery at Gettysburg.

Several thousand soldiers are buried here. A few graves are decorated with flowers, suggesting some of the dead have relatives who still come here. There's a sign at the entrance, reminding people that this is a cemetery. It says, SILENCE AND RESPECT.

Most of the tourists are being reasonably respectful, for tourists, although many, apparently without noticing, walk on the graves, stand on the bones of the soldiers.

Hardly anybody is silent. Perky tour guides are telling well-practiced stories and jokes; parents are yelling at children; children are yelling at each other.

A tour group of maybe two dozen teenagers is paying zero attention to anything but each other, flirting and laughing, wrapped in the happy self-absorbed obliviousness of TeenagerLand.

A few yards away, gazing somberly toward the teenagers, is a bust of Abraham Lincoln.

Lincoln gave his Gettysburg Address here 139 years ago, when the gentle rolling landscape, now green and manicured, was still raw and battle-scarred, the earth recently soaked with the blood of the 8,000 who died, and the tens of thousands more who were wounded, when two armies, 160,000 men, fought a terrible battle that determined the outcome of the Civil War.

Nobody planned for the battle to happen here. Neither army set out for Gettysburg.

But this is where it happened. This is where, out of randomness, out of chance, a thousand variables conspired to bring the two mighty armies together. And so this quiet little town, because it happened to be here, became historic, significant, a symbol, its identity indelibly defined by this one overwhelming event. This is where these soldiers — soldiers from Minnesota, soldiers from Kentucky, soldiers who had never heard of Gettysburg before they came here to die — will lie forever.

This is hallowed ground.

★ ★ ★

On the same July day, a few hours' drive to the west, near the small Pennsylvania town of Shanksville, Wally Miller, coroner of Somerset County, walks slowly through the tall grass covering a quiet field, to a place near the edge, just before some woods.

This is the place where, on September 11, 2001, United Airlines Flight 93, scene of a desperate airborne battle pitting passengers and crew against terrorist hijackers, came hurtling out of the sky, turning upside down and slamming into the earth at more than 500 miles an hour. That horrendous event transformed this quiet field into a smoking, reeking hell, a nightmare landscape of jet fuel, burning plane debris, scattered human remains.

Now, ten months later, the field is green again. Peaceful and green.

Except where Flight 93 plunged into the ground. That one place is still barren dirt.

That one place has not healed.

"Interesting that the grass won't grow right here," says Miller.

Nobody on Flight 93 was heading for Somerset County that day. The thirty-three passengers and seven crew members were heading from Newark to San Francisco. The four hijackers had a different destination in mind, probably Washington, possibly the White House.

Nobody on the plane meant to come here.

"I doubt that any one of them would ever set foot in Somerset County, except maybe to stop at Howard Johnson's on the turnpike," Miller says. "They have no roots here."

But this is where they are. And this is where they will stay.

No bodies were recovered here, at least not as we normally think of bodies. In the cataclysmic violence of the crash, the people on Flight 93 literally disintegrated.

Searchers found fragments of bones, small pieces of flesh, a hand. But no bodies.

In the grisly accounting of a jetliner-crash, it comes down to pounds: The people on Flight 93 weighed a total of about 7,500 pounds. Miller supervised an intensive effort to gather their remains, some flung hundreds of yards. In the end, just 600 pounds of remains were collected; of these, 250 pounds could be identified by DNA testing and returned to the families of the passengers and crew.

Forty families, wanting to bury their

loved ones. Two hundred fifty pounds of identifiable remains.

"There were people who were getting a skullcap and a tooth in the casket," Miller says. "That was their loved ones."

The rest of the remains, the vast majority, will stay here forever, in this ground.

"For all intents and purposes, they're buried here," Miller says. "This is a cemetery."

This is also hallowed ground.

In the Gettysburg Address, Lincoln was essentially trying to answer a question. The question was: How do you honor your heroes? Lincoln's answer was: You can't.

No speech you give, no monument you erect, will be worthy of them, of their sacrifice.

The best you can do is remember the cause they died for, finish the job they started.

Of course the passengers and crew on Flight 93, when they set out from Newark that morning, had no cause in common. They were people on a plane bound from Newark to San Francisco. Some were going home, some traveling on business, some on vacation.

People on a plane.

Which makes it all the more astonishing, what they did.

You've been on planes. Think how it feels, especially on a morning cross-country flight. You got up early; you're tired; you've been buckled in your seat for a couple of hours, with hours more to go. You're reading, or maybe dozing. You're essentially cargo: There's nowhere you can go, nothing you can do, no role you could possibly play in flying this huge, complex machine. You retreat into your passenger cocoon, passive, trusting your fate to the hands of others, confident that they'll get you down safe, because they always do.

Now imagine what that awful morning was like for the people on Flight 93.

Imagine being ripped from your safe little cocoon, discovering that the plane was now controlled by killers, that your life was in their bloody hands. Imagine knowing that there was nobody to help you, except you, and the people, mostly strangers, around you.

Imagine that, and ask yourself: What would you do? Could you do anything?

Could you overcome the fear clenching your stomach, the cold, paralyzing terror?

The people on Flight 93 did. With

hijackers in control of the plane, with the captain and first officer most likely dead, the people on this plane got on their cellphones and the plane's Airfones. They reached people on the ground, explained what was happening to them. They expressed their love. They said goodbye.

But they did not give up. As they were saying goodbye, they were gathering information. They learned about the World Trade Center towers. They understood that Flight 93 was on a suicide mission. They figured out what their options were.

Then they organized.

Then they fought back.

In *Among the Heroes,* a riveting book about Flight 93, *New York Times* reporter Jere Longman reports many of the last words spoken to loved ones on the ground by people on the plane. They're not the words of people in shock, people resigned to whatever fate awaits them. They're the words of people planning an attack. Fighting.

Here, for example, are the words of passenger Honor Elizabeth Wainio to her stepmother: "They're getting ready to break into the cockpit. I have to go. I love you. Goodbye."

Here are flight attendant Bradshaw's last

words to her husband:

"We're going to throw water on them and try to take the airplane over. Phil, everyone's running to first class. I've got to go. Bye."

And of course there are the now famous words of Todd Beamer, who after explaining the situation on the plane to an Airfone supervisor in Illinois, turned to somebody near him and said: "Are you guys ready? Okay, let's roll!"

They're getting ready to break into the cockpit.

I've got to go.

Let's roll.

We'll never know exactly what happened next. Some believe that the fighters managed to get into the cockpit, and that, in the ensuing struggle for control, the plane went down. Others believe that the hijackers, trying to knock the fighters off their backs, flew the plane erratically, and in doing so lost control. Inevitably, there was Internet-fueled speculation that the plane was secretly shot down by the U.S. government. (The government denies this.)

But whatever happened, we know two things for sure: We know that the plane went down before it reached its target —

that the hijackers failed to strike a national symbol, a populated area. They failed.

And we know that the people on the plane fought back. On a random day, on a random flight, they found themselves — unwarned, unprepared, unarmed — on the front lines of a vicious new kind of war. And somehow in the few confusing and terrifying minutes they had, they transformed themselves from people on a plane into soldiers, and they fought back. And that made them heroes, immediately and forever, to a wounded, angry nation, a nation that desperately wanted to fight back.

And now these heroes lie here, in this field where their battle ended.

This cemetery.

This battlefield. This hallowed ground.

Wally Miller, the coroner, has walked this ground hundreds of times. He spent endless hours among those collecting human remains and picking up plane parts. Even now, he walks with his eyes down, looking, looking. Every now and then he reaches down and picks up a tiny piece of plane — a thimble-sized piece of twisted gray metal, a bit of charred plastic, a shard of circuit board, a wire. This is what Flight 93 became: millions of tiny pieces, a vast puzzle that can never be reassembled. Despite the cleanup effort, there are still thousands of plane parts scattered for acres around the crash site, just under the new plant growth, reminders of what happened here.

The site is peaceful; no sound but birds. Miller walks from the bright field into the hemlock woods just beyond the barren spot where Flight 93 slammed into the earth. It's mid-afternoon, but the woods are in permanent dusk, the tall trees allowing only a dim, gloomy light to filter down to the lush green ferns that blanket the ground.

The woods look undisturbed, except for bright "X"s painted on the trunks of dozens of hemlocks.

The "X"s mark the trees that were scaled by climbers retrieving human remains, flung high and deep into woods by the force of the crash.

Some of the hemlocks, damaged by debris and fire and jet fuel, had to be cut down. These trees were supposed to be trucked away, but Miller, who, as coroner, still controls the crash site, would not allow it. Some of the trees have been ground into mulch; some lie in piles of logs and branches. But they're all still here.

Miller won't let them be removed.

"This is a cemetery," he says, again. And he is determined that it will be respected as a cemetery. All of it. Even the trees.

Almost immediately after the Battle of Gettysburg, people started coming to see the place where history happened. More than a century later, they're coming still.

Some are pilgrims: For them, Gettysburg is a solemn place, where the suffering and sacrifice of the soldiers still hangs heavy in the air. Some are purely tourists: For them, Gettysburg is another attraction to visit, like the Grand Canyon, or Graceland — famous, but not particularly relevant to their everyday lives. You park, you look, you take a picture, you leave.

I think that most of the visitors to Gettysburg, even today, are some mixture of pilgrim and tourist. But as the battle has receded in time, as the scars of the war have healed, tourism clearly has come to dominate the mixture. Despite the valiant efforts of many to preserve the soul of this place, to explain to the waist-pack hordes why this ground is hallowed, Gettysburg, surrounded by motels and gift shops, accessorized by a wax museum and a miniature-golf course, is now much more a tourist attraction than a shrine.

But soldiers are still buried here. And people still come to place flowers on graves.

And the sign at the entrance to the cemetery still makes its plea: SILENCE AND RESPECT.

Immediately after September 11, people started coming to see where Flight 93 went down. The site is a little tricky to find, but they found it, and they're coming still, every day, a steady stream of people who want to be near this place. They're not allowed on the site itself, which is fenced off and guarded, so they go to the temporary memorial that has been set up by the side of a two-lane rural road overlooking the crash site, a quarter-mile away.

The *memorial* — the word seems grandiose, when you see it — is a gravel parking area, two portable toilets, two flagpoles, and a fence. The fence was erected to give people a place to hang things. Many visitors leave behind something — a cross, a hat, a medal, a patch, a T-shirt, an angel, a toy airplane, a plaque — symbols, tokens, gifts for the heroes in the ground. There are messages for the heroes, too, thousands of letters, notes, graffiti scrawls, expressing sorrow, and love, and anger, and, most often, gratitude, sometimes in yearbookish prose:

"Thanx 4 everything to the heroes of Flight 93!!"

Visitors read the messages, look at the stuff on the fence, take pictures. But mostly they stare silently across the field, toward the place where Flight 93 went down. They look like people you see at Gettysburg, staring down the sloping field where Pickett's Charge was stopped, and the tide of war changed, in a few minutes of unthinkable carnage. There is nothing, really, to see on either field now, but you find it hard to pull your eyes away, knowing, imagining, what happened there.

There will be a permanent memorial for Flight 93. The temporary one is touching in its way, a heartfelt and spontaneous tribute to the heroes. But it's also haphazard, verging on tacky. Everyone agrees that something more dignified is needed.

The official wheels are already turning: Congress has begun considering a bill to place the site in federal custody. Eventually land will be acquired: a commission will be appointed; a design will be approved.

Wally Miller frets about the memorial. He worries that, in the push to commemorate this as The Defining Moment in the War Against Terrorism, people will forget that it was also — maybe primarily — a personal tragedy for forty families. He believes that, whatever is done at the site, there should be a place set aside for the Flight 93 families to grieve in private, away from the public, the tourists, the sight-seers, the voyeurs, and what Miller calls "the metal-detector ass—."

Tim Lambert, who owns the woods where many of the remains were found, agrees that the paramount concern has to be the families.

"They are forced to live with this tragedy every day," he says. "The site itself is, for the most part, the final resting place for their loved ones. People need to remember and respect that."

One of the most heartrending quotes in *Among the Heroes* is from Deena Burnett, the widow of Flight 93 passenger Tom Burnett, who is believed to have played an active role in the battle on the plane. Burnett is describing what it's like to be the widow of a hero:

"In the beginning, everyone asked, 'Aren't you proud of him? Aren't you happy that he's a hero?' I thought, my goodness, the first thing you have to understand is, I'm just trying to put one foot in front of the other. For my husband to be anyone's hero . . .

"I'd much prefer him to be here with me."

So we need to remember this: The heroes of Flight 93 were people on a plane. Their glory is being paid for, day after day, by grief. Tom Burnett does not belong to the nation. He is, first and foremost, Deena Burnett's husband, and the father of their three daughters. Any effort we make to claim him as ours is an affront to those who loved him, those he loved.

He is not ours.

And yet . . . and yet he is a hero to us, he and the other people on Flight 93. We want to honor them, just as we want to honor the firefighters, police officers, and civilians at the World Trade Center and the Pentagon who risked, and sometimes gave, their lives to try to rescue others. We want to honor them for what they did, and for reminding us that this nation is nowhere near as soft and selfish as we had come to believe.

We want to honor them.

And so in a few years, when grass grows once again over the place where Flight 93 hit the ground, when the "X"s have faded from the hemlocks, there will be a memorial here, an official, permanent memorial to the heroes of Flight 93. It will be dedicated in a somber and dignified ceremony, and people will make speeches. Somebody — bet on it — will quote the Gettysburg Address, the part about giving the last full measure of devotion. The speeches will be moving, but they will also prove Lincoln's point that the words of the living can add nothing to the deeds of the dead.

Thanx 4 everything to the heroes of Flight 93!!

There will be expressions of condolence to the families, and these, too, will be heartfelt. But they will not take away the grief.

I'd much prefer him to be here with me.

And then the ceremony will end, and the people will go home. And the heroes, the people on the plane, will remain here in the ground of Somerset County.

And years will pass, and more people will come here, and more, people who were not yet born when Flight 93 went down, coming to see this famous place.

Let's hope, for their sake, that the world they live in is less troubled than it is today. Let's hope they've never had to feel anything like the pain of September 11, 2001.

Let's also hope that, when they stand here, they know enough to be silent, to show respect.

Let's hope they understand why this is hallowed ground.

Conclusion

I was gratified by the response to the two essays about September 11. Hundreds of readers wrote nice letters, thanking me and urging me to write more often about serious topics. I appreciated their sentiments, but, as I told many of them, I'd rather not write about serious topics, because when I do, it's usually because something seriously bad has happened.

No, I'm happier writing about stupid topics, like low-flow toilets, names for rock bands, and the federal government. My journalism goal is not to make readers think. It's to make them shoot stuff out their noses.

Because boogers are my beat.

About the Author

DAVE BARRY won the Pulitzer Prize for commentary in 1988. His columns are syndicated in more than 500 newspapers. His most recent books, *Dave Barry Is Not Taking This Sitting Down* and the novels *Big Trouble* and *Tricky Business*, were national bestsellers. He lives in Miami, Floriduh.